*Pocket*
# PRAGUE
TOP SIGHTS • LOCAL LIFE • MADE EASY

**Bridget Gleeson**

# In This Book

## QuickStart Guide

Your keys to understanding the city – we help you decide what to do and how to do it

**Need to Know**
Tips for a smooth trip

**Neighbourhoods**
What's where

## Explore Prague

The best things to see and do, neighbourhood by neighbourhood

**Top Sights**
Make the most of your visit

**Local Life**
The insider's city

## The Best of Prague

The city's highlights in handy lists to help you plan

**Best Walks**
See the city on foot

**Prague's Best...**
The best experiences

## Survival Guide

Tips and tricks for a seamless, hassle-free city experience

**Getting Around**
Travel like a local

**Essential Information**
Including where to stay

Our selection of the city's best places to eat, drink and experience:

◎ **Sights**

✖ **Eating**

🔲 **Drinking**

⭐ **Entertainment**

🔒 **Shopping**

These symbols give you the vital information for each listing:

| | |
|---|---|
| 🕿 Telephone Numbers | ♦ Family-Friendly |
| ⊙ Opening Hours | 🐾 Pet Friendly |
| P Parking | 🚌 Bus |
| 🚭 Nonsmoking | ⛴ Ferry |
| @ Internet Access | M Metro |
| 🔊 Wi-Fi Access | S Subway |
| 🥗 Vegetarian Selection | 🚋 Tram |
| 📖 English-Language Menu | 🚆 Train |

Find each listing quickly on maps for each neighbourhood:

**Bar Hemingway**

16 🔲 Map p233, B2

Legend has it that Hemi self, wielding a machine erate this timber-pan ered bar during showpiece is a en by Papa ar town. Dress s.com; Hôtel Rit ; ⊙6.30pm-2a

6 ◎ Plac
V₂

# QuickStart Guide 7

# Explore Prague 21

## Worth a Trip:

# QuickStart Guide

## Welcome to Prague

More than 20 years after the Velvet Revolution drew back the curtain on this intoxicating maze of winding cobblestone alleyways, the 'city of 100 spires' thrills visitors with dramatic Gothic architecture, cool cubist design, down-to-earth pubs, ornate cafes, cutting-edge art and the grand Prague Castle, looming high over the city and creating a spectacular sky-line that looks like it's straight out of a fairy tale.

Church of Our Lady Before Týn (p73), Old Town Sq
RACHEL LEWIS/LONELY PLANET IMAGES ©

# Prague
# Top Sights

**Prague Castle** (p24)

Looming high above the Vltava's left bank, this outrageously outsized fortress conjures up childhood fairy tales of a good king watching benevolently over his people.

RACHEL LEWIS/LONELY PLANET IMAGES ©

### St Vitus Cathedral (p30)

The Gothic centrepiece of Prague Castle is famous for its beautiful stained- and painted-glass windows, ornate chapels, and spires that seem to pierce the sky.

### Old Town Square & Astronomical Clock (p72)

The nightmarish Gothic spires of the Church of Our Lady Before Týn rise above this famous square, known in part for its Astronomical Clock, where every hour, Death rings a bell and inverts his hourglass.

### Charles Bridge (p74)

This stunning stone bridge, commissioned by Emperor Charles IV in 1357 and lined with saintly statues, provides an unforgettable passage between Prague Castle and Old Town.

### Jewish Museum (p60)

This extensive museum comprises six important sites of Prague's former Jewish ghetto, including the beautiful Spanish Synagogue.

### Jewish Cemetery (p62)

With 12,000 gravestones and some 100,000 bodies packed into a space the size of a few suburban gardens, Prague's old Jewish Cemetery is like no other on earth.

### Petřín Hill (p42)

The 318m-high grassy knoll, popular with joggers, dog-walkers, lovers and families – and immortalised by novelist Milan Kundera – offers magnificent vistas across the 'city of 100 spires'.

### Loreta (p32)

A baroque place of pilgrimage, the Loreta is noted for its cloister and chapels, a lavish diamond-studded artwork and the ancient bells that ring out over the city of Prague from its clock tower.

### Wenceslas Square (p90)

Pictured on postcards that highlight the equestrian statue of 'good king Wenceslas', the massive square was once a gathering point for proud Czechs and Velvet Revolution demonstrators.

### Veletržní Palace (p124)

Off the beaten path in the neighbourhood of Holešovice, this larger-than-life functionalist structure houses an impressive collection of avant-garde Czech art and works by European masters like Cézanne, Rodin, Klimt and Schiele.

# Prague Local Life

*Insider tips to help you find the real city*

Czechs are a cool, laid-back bunch fond of walking their dogs down to the beer garden. After you've seen the castle and walked across Charles Bridge, join the locals in their favourite parks, working-class neighbourhoods and watering holes.

## Gardens of Malá Strana (p44)

▶ Wallenstein Garden
▶ Kampa Island

In the shadows of Prague Castle, the city's 'Lesser Quarter' has a particularly high concentration of lovely parks and gardens. Do as the locals do and seek refuge in the green spaces; bring a blanket, a book, a beer and your own picnic lunch to one of these inviting urban oases.

## Drinking Tour of Vinohrady & Žižkov (p112)

▶ U Sadu
▶ Hapu

Žižkov's proud citizens claim their neighbourhood has more pubs per square metre than anywhere else in the world. Neighbouring Vinohrady is filled with fashionable cocktail lounges and wine bars. Put it together and you've got a great, boozy night out on the town in this leafy (and just slightly out-of-the-way) residential district.

## Vyšehrad, Prague's Other Castle (p108)

▶ Mucha's grave at Vyšehrad Cemetery
▶ Vyšehrad Casemates

Prague's second 'castle' is very different from its first but equally dramatic in its own right. Indeed, it's been centuries since any real castle stood here. But this ruined citadel more than atones for any architectural shortcomings with breathtaking views south of the Vltava River and north over Prague. Up here, you feel you're floating above the city.

## Alternative Art in Smíchov (p56)

▶ MeetFactory
▶ Švandovo divadlo

Though it's slowly gentrifying, this industrial neighbourhood is still known for its edgy alternative art scene, down-to-earth bars and an avant-garde theatre. It's close to the centre, just a short tram ride from Malá Strana – but it's just far enough off the beaten path to allow visitors a taste of today's 'real' Prague.

Drinking in Vinohrady

View of Vyšehrad Castle

**Other great places to experience the city like a local:**

*Tankovna* pubs (p66)

Kampa Island (p48)

Riegrovy sady (p117)

Karolíny Světlé (p81)

Scouting out SoNa (p106)

DOX Centre for Contemporary Art (p127)

Bohemian glass at Kotva (p69)

Stromovka Park (p128)

Josef Pleskot's Tunnel (p38)

# Prague
## Day Planner

## Day One

If you've only got one day in Prague, focus on the major sights. Start early, joining the crowd beneath the **Astronomical Clock** (p73) for the hourly chiming, then wander through gorgeous **Old Town Square** (p72), taking in views of a spectacular array of architectural styles and the ominous spires of our **Church of Our Lady Before Týn** (p73). Stop for coffee and chocolate croissants at the charming **Bakeshop Praha** (p65) before making a short visit to the historic **Jewish Cemetery** (p62) in the city's one-time Jewish ghetto.

Enjoy a stroll through the winding cobblestone alleyways of Old Town on your way to one of Prague's most famous landmarks, **Charles Bridge** (p74). While crossing over the massive stone bridge, stop to take photos of the Vltava River, the ancient gates and the magnificent **Prague Castle** (p24) looming high over the fairy-tale scene. Spend the afternoon visiting **St Vitus Cathedral** (p30) and the castle's formal gardens, exhibits and palaces.

Do as the locals do – go for goulash and beer at a Czech microbrewery like **Kolkovna** (p66) or relax at a traditional cafe such as **Café Louvre** (p105).

## Day Two

Spend the morning exploring the quaint backstreets and leafy public gardens of Prague's Malá Strana or 'Lesser Quarter', one of the city's oldest districts. Catch the **Petřín Funicular** (p43) and enjoy sweeping views from the hilltop park. Then head downhill along picturesque **Nerudova** (p48), stopping into elegant **Wallenstein Garden** (p44) to take a break among the flowers. Laugh at the **Piss sculpture** (p45) at Cihelná before treating yourself to lunch at the lovely riverside **Hergetova Cihelná** (p49).

Cross the river via Mánes Bridge. Check out the famous synagogues of the **Jewish Museum** (p60), then take a break with coffee and chocolate cake on the sunny balcony of the striking cubist **Grand Café Orient** (p81).

Stop by the box office of the **National Theatre** (p106) to see if any last-minute tickets are available to the opera or ballet. Before the show, have a coffee or champagne at one-time literary hot spot **Kavárna Slavia** (p105); you'll have to fight for one of the prized tables facing Prague Castle. After the curtain call, go for a classy nightcap at **Tretter's New York Bar** (p66) or **Bar & Books** (p81).

**Short on time?**
We've arranged Prague's must-sees into these day-by-day itineraries to make sure you see the very best of the city in the time you have available.

## Day Three

In the morning, cross Charles Bridge and head south into **Kampa Island** (p48) for fresh air and river views. Take the funicular up **Petřín Hill** (p43) and walk to **Strahov Monastery** (p35). If you haven't had enough time to enjoy Prague Castle's various attractions and exhibits, head back – the changing of the guard at the castle's main gate at noon is a sight to be seen. Have a coffee on the terrace at **Lobkowicz Palace Café** (p37).

Have a leisurely lunch at **U zlaté hrušky** (p37) then stop at the **Loreta** (p32) to hear the clock tower's famous bells ring and see the diamond-studded Prague Sun in the treasury. Treat yourself to a local beer at classic nearby pub **U Černého vola** (p38).

If it's not dark out yet, head to Wenceslas Square and the nearby sights – the **Jan Palach Memorial** (p91), the **Wenceslas Statue** (p91), **Lucerna Passage** (p93) and the **cubist lamppost** (p93). To drink cocktails and dance with the beautiful people, head to **M1 Lounge** (p66); for something a little more rock and roll, head to the **Roxy** (p69). If you're up for some authentic nightlife, take tram 1, 3 or 5 north across the river to Holešovice for **Cross Club** (p128) or **SaSaZu** (p129).

## Day Four

Have a grand breakfast at **Café Savoy** (p49). Check what's on at the **State Opera House** (p97) and reserve seats for tonight if possible. Then shop for picnic supplies at **Country Life** (p81) or **Tesco** (p107) and board the metro to **Vyšehrad** (p108). After wandering around the ruins and visiting the graves of Dvořak and Mucha in the cemetery, you'll be ready for a picnic on Vyšehrad's clifftop.

Head to Vinohrady and Žižkov. Admire the **Church of the Most Sacred Heart of Our Lord** (p116) and wander to the base of the nearby **Žižkov Tower** (p116) to look at the giant babies crawling up it. If you're thirsty, check out a couple of the stops along our **Drinking Tour of Vinohrady & Žižkov** (p112). Catch a tram to **Veletržní Palace** (p124; the quickest route is a Line A metro to Malostranská, then tram 12) to see one of the city's great art collections.

Wander over to **Letná Gardens** (p127) to enjoy a Gambrinus in the beer garden as the sun sets on this magnificent city. Proceed to the State Opera if you were lucky enough to score tickets. If not, try cocktails on the rooftop terrace of the **Hotel U Prince** (p78). It's unabashedly touristy, but you'll never forget the glittering views over Old Town Sq.

# Need to Know

For more information, see Survival
Guide (p157)

................................................

**Currency**
Czech crown (Koruna česká; Kč)

................................................

**Language**
Czech

................................................

**Visas**
Generally not required for stays of up to
three months.

................................................

**Money**
ATMs are widely available and credit cards
are accepted at many restaurants and
hotels across the city.

................................................

**Mobile Phones**
The Czech Republic uses GSM 900,
compatible with mobile phones from the
rest of Europe, Australia and New Zealand
but not with most North American phones.

................................................

**Time**
Central European Time (GMT plus one hour)

................................................

**Plugs & Adaptors**
Most plugs have two round pins; electrical
current is 230V. North American travellers
will need adaptors and, depending on the
device, transformers.

................................................

**Tipping**
It's standard practice in pubs, cafes and
midrange restaurants to add between
10% and 15% if service has been good.
In a taxi, round up the fare.

## 1 Before You Go

### Your Daily Budget

#### Budget less than €50
▶ Dorm beds €10–20
▶ Excellent supermarkets for self-catering
▶ Cheap theatre tickets at the best venues
starting at just €4

#### Midrange €50–150
▶ Dinner for two with local beer/wine €20–40
▶ Double room at midrange boutique hotel
€100

#### Top end more than €150
▶ Double room or suite at luxury hotel
€150–225
▶ Four-course dinner at Kampa Park €150

### Useful Websites

**Lonely Planet** (www.lonelyplanet.com/czech
-republic/prague) Destination information,
hotel bookings, traveller forum and more.

**Prague Welcome** (www.praguewelcome.cz)
Prague's official tourism portal.

**Prague.com** (www.prague.com) A city guide
plus hotel bookings.

**Heart of Europe** (www.heartofeurope.cz)
Lists cultural events, concerts, clubs, theatres, museums and galleries.

### Advance Planning

**One month before** Reserve your hotel
room, especially if you're hoping to stay in a
smaller B&B or boutique hotel.

**One week before** Get theatre tickets if you
want to see a specific performance.

**One day before** Check the Prague Castle
website (www.hrad.cz) to find out about
the next day's cultural events.

## ② Arriving in Prague

Most visitors to Prague will enter via the international airport, Prague-Ruzyně, or through the main train station, Praha hlavň nádraží. Public transport and private taxis are easily available from both hubs. See p160 for more information on the public buses, shuttles and taxis listed here.

### ✈ Prague-Ruzyně Airport

| Destination | Best Transport |
|---|---|
| Old Town | Cedaz Shuttlebus to Náměstí Republiky |
| Hradčany | Taxi or bus 119 to metro station Dejvická, connection to Hradčanská metro station |
| Malá Strana | Taxi or bus 119 to metro station Dejvická, connection to Malostranská metro station |
| Wenceslas Sq | Airport Express bus to hlavní nádraží train station area |
| Vinohrady & Žižkov | Taxi or bus 119 to metro station Dejvická, connection to Jiřiho z Podebrad metro station |

### 🚆 Praha hlavň nádraží Train Station

| Destination | Best Transport |
|---|---|
| Old Town | Walk or take metro Line A to Staroměstská station |
| Hradčany | Metro Line A to Hradčanská station |
| Malá Strana | Metro Line A to Malostranská station |
| Wenceslas Sq | Walk (it's two blocks away) |
| Vinohrady & Žižkov | Metro Line A to Jiřiho z Podebrad station |

## ③ Getting Around

Prague's public transport system is affordable and efficient, and one of Europe's best. Most visitors will get everywhere they need to go by walking, taking the metro, or hopping on a tram.

### Ⓜ Metro

Prague's metro system runs from 5am to midnight with fast, frequent service. For tourists, the most useful line is A (green), which runs from Dejvická (airport connection) to Prague Castle, Malá Strana, Old Town Sq, Wenceslas Sq and Žižkov/ Vinohrady.

### 🚋 Tram

Travelling on the antique red trams in Prague is part of the cultural experience. Regular trams run from 5am to midnight. Important tram lines to remember are 22 (runs to Prague Castle, Malá Strana and Charles Bridge); 17 and 18 (run to the Jewish Quarter and Old Town Sq); and 11 (to Žižkov and Vinohrady). After midnight night trams (51 to 58) rumble across the city about every 40 minutes.

### 🚕 Taxi

Taxis are a convenient option when you're in a hurry, but be careful of scams. Look for the 'Taxi Fair Place' stations in key tourist areas: drivers can charge a maximum fare and must announce the estimated price in advance. Make sure you know the current exchange rate if the driver offers you the chance to pay in a foreign currency.

# Prague Neighbourhoods

## Prague Castle & Hradčany (p22)

This refined hilltop district is dominated by the castle that gives Prague its dreamy, fairy-tale-like appearance.

**◉ Top Sights**

Prague Castle

St Vitus Cathedral

Loreta

## Jewish Museum & Josefov (p58)

Today the city's one-time Jewish ghetto is home to a cluster of historic synagogues and the eerie, beautiful Jewish Cemetery.

**◉ Top Sights**

Jewish Museum

Jewish Cemetery

## Petřín Hill & Malá Strana (p40)

Quaint cobblestoned streets, red roofs, ancient cloisters and a peaceful hillside park characterise Prague's charming 'Lesser Quarter'.

**◉ Top Sights**

Petřín Hill

## Old Town Square & Staré Město (p70)

Gothic spires, art-nouveau architecture, a quirky astronomical clock and horse-drawn carriages crowd this famous, colourful old square.

**◉ Top Sights**

Old Town Square & Astronomical Clock

Charles Bridge

## Wenceslas Square & Around (p88)

Once a horse market, this huge square has been the site of seminal moments in Czech history.

**◉ Top Sights**

Wenceslas Square

St Vitus Cathedral

Prague Castle

Loreta

Jewish Cemetery

Jewish Museum

Charles Bridge

Old Town Square & Astronomical Clock

Petřín Hill

*Veletržní Palace*

**Holešovice (p122)**
Beer gardens, contemporary art and huge parks characterise this laid-back district well off the tourist path.

**Top Sights**
Veletržní Palace

*Wenceslas Square*

**Nové Město (p100)**
Cool modern architecture and quiet riverside cafes are the crowning glories of this underrated neighbourhood.

**Vinohrady & Žižkov (p110)**
The locals' residential neighbourhood of choice, this leafy area contains many of Prague's hippest bars and cafes.

# Explore
# **Prague**

Charles Bridge (p74) and Old Town Bridge Tower
RICHARD NEBESKY/LONELY PLANET IMAGES ©

Explore

# Prague Castle & Hradčany

The spires of St Vitus Cathedral, rising up from the heart of Prague Castle, are rarely out of view when you're wandering around the city. In Hradčany (the castle district), visitors are particularly conscious of the royal omnipresence; passing through the doll-sized alleyways, you'll have an idea what life was like for the castle's hard-working medieval minions.

RICHARD NEBESKY/LONELY PLANET IMAGES ©

# The Sights in a Day

Get up early and make your way to the main entrance of **Prague Castle** (p24) just before 9am. After choosing a ticket type (long or short tour) at the information centre, head straight for **St Vitus Cathedral** (p30) to check out the magnificent church before the big crowds show up. Visit the **Old Royal Palace** (p25) and peruse the art collection at **St George's Convent** (p29) before taking a break in the **Royal Garden** (p27). Make your way back to the **castle entrance** (p25) for the changing of the guard at noon.

After a lunch break, walk down to the **Loreta** (p32) and take the audio tour of the major sights, including **Santa Casa** (p33) and the **Church of the Nativity of Our Lord** (p33). Make sure to pay attention at the turn of the hour – you won't want to miss the ringing of the famous **Carillon** church bells. Then stop at one of the cafes around Loreta Sq.

If it's before 5pm, take a break from royal and religious themes at the quirky **Miniatures Museum** (p36). Before dinner, wander the charming streets of **Nový Svět Quarter** (p35).

## Top Sights

Prague Castle (p24)

St Vitus Cathedral (p30)

Loreta (p32)

## Best of Prague

**Food**

U zlaté hrušky (p37)

Malý Buddha (p38)

Lobkowicz Palace Café (p37)

**Art**

Prague Castle Picture Gallery (p29)

Schwarzenberg Palace (p35)

Mucha's painted windows (p31)

**For Free**

Prague Castle (p24)

Nový Svět Quarter (p35)

**History**

Tomb of St John of Nepomuk (p31)

Prague Sun (p33)

St Vitus Cathedral (p30)

## Getting There

🚋 **Tram** Take 22 to Pražský hrad then walk five minutes, or to Pohořelec then walk downhill.

Ⓜ **Metro** Take Line A to Malostranská, then climb the steps.

# Top Sights
## Prague Castle

Known simply as *hrad* to proud Czechs, Prague Castle was founded by 9th-century Přemysl princes and grew haphazardly as subsequent rulers made additions. Today it's a huge complex, larger than seven football fields, proceeding west to east through a series of three courtyards. There have been four major reconstructions. All Czech rulers have had their residence here, except the first post-communist president, Václav Havel: in 1989 he plumped for the comforts of his own home instead.

◉ Map p34, D2

www.hrad.cz

Pražský hrad

long/short tour adult 350/250Kč, concession 175/125Kč

🕙9am-6pm Apr-Oct, to 4pm Nov-Mar

🚊 to Pohořelec

Vladislav Hall in Prague Castle

# Don't Miss

## Castle Entrance

The castle's main gate, on Hradčany Sq, is flanked by huge, 18th-century statues of battling Titans that dwarf the guards below. Playwright-turned-president Václav Havel hired the Czech costume designer on the film *Amadeus* to redesign the guards' uniforms and instigated a changing-of-the-guard ceremony – the most impressive display is at noon.

## Golden Lane

The tiny, colourful cottages along this cobbled alley, recently reopened after extensive renovations, were built in the 16th century for the castle guard's sharpshooters, but were later used by goldsmiths, squatters and artists, including writer Franz Kafka (who stayed at his sister's house at No 22 from 1916 to 1917).

## Old Royal Palace

The palace's highlight is the high Gothic vaulted roof of Vladislav Hall (Vladislavský sál; 1493–1502), beneath which all the presidents of the Czech Republic have been sworn in. There's also a balcony off the hall with great city views and a door to the former Bohemian Chancellery (České kanceláře), where the so-called Second Defenestration of Prague occurred in 1618.

## Rosenberg Palace

Originally built as the grand residence of the Rosenberg family, this 16th-century Renaissance-style palace was later repurposed by Empress Maria Theresa as a 'Residence for Noblewomen'. The institute housed 30 unmarried women at a time; today, one section of the palace recreates the style of an 18th-century noblewoman's

☑ **Top Tips**

▶ The castle opens at 9am; be there a few minutes before to beat the crowds.

▶ You'll need at least half a day to explore the castle grounds.

▶ Join an official hour-long tour (400Kč, in English and other languages) leaving from the information centres. Book ahead in summer by emailing tourist.info@hrad.cz.

▶ To catch a concert on castle grounds, stop at the ticket desk at the second courtyard's information centre; also check out www.jazznahrade.cz for info on the free 'Jazz at the Castle' series.

✕ **Take a Break**

Stop for coffee or lunch at the lovely new Lobkowicz Palace Café (p37), located on the ground level of Lobkowicz Palace in the castle complex.

If you'd rather step outside the castle walls, enjoy gorgeous views with your coffee at Bellavista (p38).

# Prague Castle

JOHN ELK III/LONELY PLANET IMAGES ©

Old Castle Steps

Lobkowicz Palace Café

Lobkowicz Palace

Rosenberg Palace

Golden Lane

St George's Convent

St George's Basilica

Royal Garden

St George's Square

Story of Prague Castle

Old Royal Palace

Southern Gardens

St Vitus Cathedral

Third Courtyard

Plečník Monolith

Information Centre

Second Courtyard

Prague Castle Picture Gallery

Information Centre

New Castle Steps

First Courtyard

Castle Entrance

Hradčany Sq

Second courtyard, Prague Castle

apartment using artefacts (lamps, porcelain, candlesticks and furniture) from the Prague Castle's depository.

### Plečník Monolith
In the third courtyard, a noteworthy feature near St Vitus Cathedral is a huge granite monolith dedicated to the victims of WWI, designed by Slovene architect Jože Plečník in 1928. Nearby is a copy of the castle's famous statue of St George slaying the dragon.

### Royal Garden
Powder Bridge (Prašný most; 1540) spans the Stag Moat (Jelení příkop) en route to the spacious Renaissance-style Royal Garden, dating from 1534.

The most beautiful building is the Ball-Game House (Míčovna; 1569), a masterpiece of Renaissance sgraffito where the Habsburgs once played badminton. East is the Summer Palace (Letohrádek; 1538–60) and west the former Riding School (jízdárna; 1695).

### Southern Gardens
The three gardens lined up below the castle's southern wall – Paradise Garden, the Hartig Garden and the Garden on the Ramparts – offer superb views over Malá Strana's rooftops. Approach this contiguous bit of greenery from the west via the New Castle Steps or from the east via the Old Castle Steps.

## Understand
## Kings & Castles

Prague's royal history, characterised by people throwing themselves out of castle windows and men burning each other at the stake, makes *The Tudors* look tame.

### In the Beginning
The name Bohemia, still used to describe the western Czech Republic, comes from Celtic tribe the Boii, who lived in the area that later became Prague around 400 BC. Later, in the 6th century, two Slavic tribes arrived – with the 'Czechs' building a wooden fortress near the current castle, and the Zličani settling at Vyšehrad. The 9th-century Přemysl dynasty not only built the earliest section of today's Prague Castle in the 9th century, but also included one Václav, or Wenceslas, of 'Good King' carol fame.

### The Golden Age
After the Přemysls died out and Prague came under the direct rule of Holy Roman Emperor Charles IV (1316–78), the city blossomed. During this 'golden age', Charles – whose mother was Czech – elevated Prague's official status and went on a building spree, founding the New Town (Nové Město), Charles Bridge, Charles University and adding St Vitus Cathedral to the castle.

One of the university's rectors, Jan Hus, led the 15th-century Hussite movement, which challenged the Catholic Church and its corruption. Hus was famously burned at the stake in 1415 for his reformist 'heresy', but his death kicked off decades of internecine fighting that eventually put Hussites in charge for several decades.

### Habsburg Rule
In 1526 Czech lands came under the rule of the Austrian Habsburgs. With the Reformation in full swing in Europe, tensions between Catholic Habsburgs and reformist Czechs inevitably surfaced. In 1618 Bohemian rebels threw two Catholic councillors from a Prague Castle window sparking the Europe-wide Thirty Years' War (1618–48). Following a defeat of the Czech nobility in 1620 at the Battle of White Mountain (Bílá Hora) the Czechs lost their independence for nearly 300 years.

### St George's Basilica
Behind a brick-red facade lies the Czech Republic's best-preserved Romanesque church. The original was established in the 10th century by Vratislav I (the father of St Wenceslas), who is still buried here, as is St Ludmilla. All in all, it's mostly popular for small concert performances.

### Story of Prague Castle
One of the castle's newest and most compelling **exhibitions** (adult/concession 140/70Kč) displaying an outstanding collection of armour, jewellery, glassware, furniture and other artefacts from more than 1000 years of castle history. One outstanding sight is the skeleton of the pre-Christian 'warrior', still encased in the earth where archaeologists found him within the castle grounds.

### St George's Convent
Bohemia's first convent was established in 973, and now contains a branch of the National Gallery, featuring an excellent collection of 19th-century Bohemian paintings. The former home of Benedictine nuns also displays sculpture, silver, clothing, furniture and porcelain.

### Lobkowicz Palace
The only privately owned building in the Prague Castle complex, this 16th-century aristocratic **palace** (Lobkowicz Palace adult/concession 275/200Kč) reopened in 2007 with a collection of Renaissance paintings, musical instruments and some manuscripts by Mozart and Beethoven. Among the paintings are one of Velázquez's *Infantas* and Pieter Brueghel the Elder's *Haymaking*.

### Prague Castle Picture Gallery
In 1648 an invading Swedish army looted Emperor Rudolf II's art collection (as well as making off with the original bronze statues in the Wallenstein Garden). These converted Renaissance stables house what was left plus replacement works, including some by Rubens, Tintoretto and Titian.

## Top Sights
# St Vitus Cathedral

The largest and most noteworthy church in the Czech Republic was begun in 1344. Though it appears Gothic to the very tips of its pointy spires, much of St Vitus Cathedral was only completed in time for its belated consecration in 1929. The coronations of Bohemia's kings were held here through the mid-19th century. Today it's the seat of the Archbishop of Prague and the final resting place of some of the nation's most illustrious figures – kings, princes, even saints.

👁 Map p34, D2

Prague Castle complex

admission free

🕑 9am-4pm Mon-Sat, from noon Sun

🚊 to Pohořelec or Pražský hrad

Eastern towers, St Vitus Cathedral

# Don't Miss

### Golden Gate

The main entrance features a breathtaking gilded 14th-century mosaic depicting the Last Judgment.

### Chapel of St Wenceslas

This chapel, considered the centre of St Vitus Cathedral, houses the tomb of a famous provincial saint. But the ornate 14th-century decorations are more interesting – including walls inlaid with precious stones, large Passion cycle paintings, and scenes from the life of the Bohemian duke Wenceslas, who was killed at the hands of his own brother in the year 935.

### Royal Oratory

Kings addressed their subjects from this grand, intricately crafted oratory that appears to be woven with gnarled tree branches. Dating from 1493, it's a striking centrepiece to the cathedral and exemplifies late-Gothic aesthetics.

### Mucha's Painted-Glass Windows

Adding a modern twist to the historic cathedral, world-famous 20th-century art-nouveau painter Alfons Mucha contributed painted-glass windows to the north wall. The vibrant hues and lifelike figures are easy to recognise; the crowded scene depicts the blessing of SS Cyril and Methodius.

### Tomb of St John of Nepomuk

Nepomuk was a priest and a religious martyr; it's said that hundreds of years after his death, when his body was exhumed, his tongue was found 'still alive'. The Church canonised him and commissioned this elaborate silver sarcophagus for his reburial. (Scientists later showed that the red tissue, or 'tongue', was actually a part of his brain congealed in blood.)

RICHARD NEBESKY/LONELY PLANET IMAGES ©

## ☑ Top Tips

▸ Visit St Vitus Cathedral first thing in the morning, when the crowds are smaller.

▸ If you want to photograph interiors, look for the desk inside the cathedral's entrance – for 50Kč, they'll give you a temporary permit to take nonflash photos.

▸ For spectacular views, climb the stairway to the cathedral's tower (included with Prague Castle admission.)

▸ To attend a service here, inquire at the information centres for times.

## ✕ Take a Break

Take a healthful lunch break, or enjoy a steaming cup of jasmine tea, at Malý Buddha (p38), a short walk from the castle's main entrance.

Leaving the castle complex? Stop for a coffee at U zavěšenýho kafe (p39) on your way down the hill.

## Top Sights
# Loreta

A crucified and bearded lady, a famous clock tower, a cloister, fabulous jewels, the skeletons of two Spanish saints – all can be found in one location at this baroque place of pilgrimage. Financed by the Lobkowitz family, the structure was started in 1626. Loreta is named after the town in Italy where the Holy House (the Virgin Mary's home in Nazareth, said to have flown to Italy with the help of angels in the 13th century) is located.

👁 Map p34, B3

www.loreta.cz

Loretánské náměstí 7

adult/concession
130/100Kč

🕑9am-5pm Apr-Oct,
9.30am-4pm Nov-Mar

🚋22 to Pohořelec

Loreta

# Don't Miss

### Prague Sun

The Loreta's eye-popping treasury boasts a star attraction – a dazzling object called the Prague Sun. Studded with 6222 diamonds, it was a gift to the Loreta from Countess Ludmila of Kolowrat. In her will she wrote that the piece must be crafted from her personal collection of diamonds – wedding gifts from her third husband.

### Santa Casa

Italian for 'Holy House,' this brick structure is loosely based on the Italian original. Surrounded by a courtyard and six chapels, it features a Virgin Mary statue from the early 17th century, fading frescos, and relief sculptures from Mary's life, focusing in particular on her days of young motherhood. The Prague Archbishop consecrated the house in 1631.

### Church of the Nativity of Our Lord

A noble family of architects was behind the construction of this church, perhaps the most important chapel in the Prague Loreta. Completed in 1738, the chapel contains impressive cherub sculptures, replicas of Renaissance paintings, side altars with rococo depictions of saints, an antique organ, and frescos showing the nativity and the adoration of the Magi.

### Carillon

The peal of these church bells – meant to be an hourly call to prayer – is a symbol of Prague itself. The rare bells were given as a gift to the Loreto in the late 17th century; after consecration, they were placed in the clock tower to great fanfare. They first rang out over the city on 15 August 1695.

RICHARD MASBSKY/LONELY PLAN

## ☑ Top Tips

▶ The worthwhile audio guide, available in several languages, costs 150Kč.

▶ Sometimes the souvenir shop is closed; you can ask at the cashier's desk to buy postcards and guides.

▶ Families (two adults and up to five children under 16) can ask for the 270Kč family rate.

▶ If you'd like to take photos (no flash or tripod allowed), ask for a permit (100Kč).

## ✕ Take a Break

Kick back with a pint of icy Czech beer at atmospheric pub U Černého vola (p38).

Before or after touring the Loreta, treat yourself to a first-class lunch or dinner in the garden at local favourite U zlaté hrušky (p37).

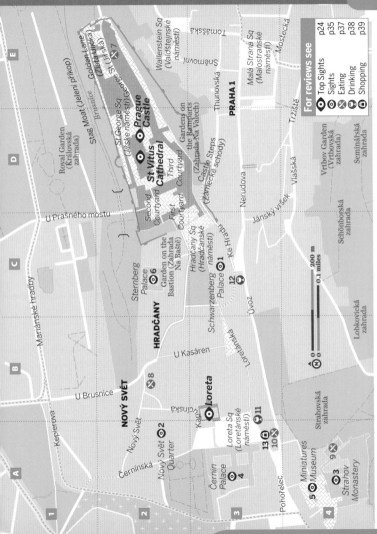

Royal Garden (Královská zahrada)

Stag Moat (Jelení příkop)

Golden Lane (Zlatá Ulička)

George St (Jiřská) ✗ 7

St George Sq (Jiřské náměstí)

Brusnice

Wallenstein Sq (Valdštejnské náměstí)

Tomášská

Sněmovní

Prague Castle

St Vitus Cathedral ◎

Third Courtyard

Gardens on the Ramparts (Zahrada Na Valech)

Thunovská

Malá Strana Sq (Malostranské náměstí)

Mostecká

Second Courtyard

First Courtyard

Castle Steps (Zámecké schody)

PRAHA 1

Tržiště

U Prašného mostu

Mariánské hradby

Sternberg Palace ◎ 6

Garden on the Bastion (Zahrada Na Baště)

Hradčany Sq (Hradčanské náměstí) ◎

Nerudova

Jánský vršek

Vlašská

Vrbov Garden (Vrtbovská zahrada)

Schönbornská zahrada

Seminářská zahrada

Keplerova

HRADČANY

Schwarzenberg Palace ◎ 1

◎ 12
◉

Ke Hradu

Úvoz

Loretánská

200 m
0.1 miles

Lobkovická zahrada

U Kasáren

NOVÝ SVĚT

✗ 8

U Brusnice

Loreta ◎

Kap_cínská

◉ 11

Nový Svět ◎ 2

Nový Svět Quarter

Loreta Sq (Loretánské náměstí)

13 ◉
10 ✗

Strahovská zahrada

Černínská

Čern_n Palace ◎ 4

Miniatures Museum ◎

◎ 5

✗ 9

◎ 3

Strahov Monastery

Pohořelec

# Sights

## Schwarzenberg Palace

HISTORIC SITE

1  Map p34, C3

Hradčany Sq, at Prague Castle's main gates, is dominated by the striking black-and-white *sgraffito* facade of this 18th-century palace. Part of the National Gallery, the collection features more than 400 examples of sculpture and painting from the Renaissance and late-baroque periods. (Schwarzenberský palác; www.ngprague.cz; adult/concession 250/120Kč; ⏰10am-6pm Tue-Sun)

## Nový Svět Quarter

HISTORIC AREA

2  Map p34, A2

In the 16th century, houses were built for castle staff in an enclave of curving cobblestone streets down the slope to the north of the Loreta. Today these diminutive cottages have been restored and painted in pastel shades, making the 'New World' Quarter into a perfect alternative to the castle's crowded Golden Lane. The Danish astronomer Tycho Brahe (see p82) lived at No 1 Kapucínská. (Nový Svět, Černínská & around; 🚊22 to Brusnice)

## Strahov Monastery

CHURCH

3  Map p34, A4

Apart from having magnificent views over Prague, Strahov Monastery's main drawcard is the baroque

**Strahov Library** (Strahovská knihovna). This is divided into two magnificent book-lined halls – the two-storey high **Philosophy Hall** (Filozofický sál; 1780–97), with its grandiose ceiling fresco, and the stucco-encrusted **Theology Hall** (Teologiský sál; 1679). For conservation reasons you can only peek through the doors, but the connecting hall also contains a **Cabinet of Curiosities** full of shrivelled sea creatures. (Strahovský klášter; www.strahovskyklaster.cz; Strahovské nádvoří 1; adult/concession 80/50Kč; ⏰9am-noon & 1-5pm; 🚊22 to Pohořelec)

---

☑ Top Tip

**Visiting Prague Castle**

Tickets to Prague Castle are valid for two days, although you may visit each attraction only once. Additional attractions levy separate entry fees.

**The long tour** (adult/concession 350/175Kč) Includes Old Royal Palace, Story of Prague Castle, St George's Basilica, St George's Convent, Golden Lane with Daliborka Tower, Prague Castle Picture Gallery

**The short tour** (adult/concession 250/125Kč) Includes Old Royal Palace, Story of Prague Castle, St George's Basilica, Golden Lane with Daliborka Tower

RICHARD NEBESKÝ/LONELY PLANET IMAGES ©

National Gallery at Sternberg Palace

### Černin Palace

HISTORIC SITE

4 ⊙ Map p34, A3

Prague is infamous for defenestrations in which hapless political opponents have hurtled from windows. One occurred here. In 1948 Jan Masaryk – son of first Czechoslovak president Tomáš Masaryk and the only noncommunist in the postwar government – 'fell' to his death from his top-floor bathroom. Used as SS headquarters during WWII, the 17th-century building now houses the foreign ministry.

### Miniatures Museum

MUSEUM

5 ⊙ Map p34, A4

This collection of miniature artworks remains one of Prague's quirky gems. Peer through microscopes to see a flea with golden horseshoes and tiny camels biblically passing through the eye of a needle. Alternatively, raise a magnifying glass to miniature reproduction paintings and the world's smallest book, painstakingly created by Siberian optical technician Anatoly Konyenko over many years. (Muzeum miniatur; Strahov Monastery; adult/child 50/30Kč; ⊙10am-5pm; 🚊22 to Pohořelec)

### Sternberg Palace

MUSEUM

6 ⊙ Map p34, C2

Right on Hradčany's main square, this palace is home to one of the National Gallery's collections of 14th- to 18th-century European art, including works by Breughel, Dürer,

Goya, Rembrandt and Rubens. There's an appealing cafe on-site. (Šternbersky Palác; www.ngprague.cz; Hradčanské náměstí 15; adult/concession 150/80Kč; ⏱10am-6pm Tue-Sun)

# Eating

## Lobkowicz Palace Café CAFE €

 7 Map p34, E2

A convenient stop while touring Prague Castle, this elegant new cafe on the ground level of Lobkowicz Palace offers tasty sandwiches and pastries, Czech dishes, plus coffee, wine and beer. The best tables are on the balcony – with views over Malá Strana – or, in warmer weather, in the pretty courtyard. (Lobkowicz Palace; mains 85-150Kč; ⏱10am-6pm; 🚋22 to Pohořelec; 🛜 👶)

## U Zlaté Hrušky CZECH €€€

8 Map p34, B2

Treat yourself to beautifully prepared Czech and international dishes at this fastidious restaurant in the romantic Nový Svět Quarter. 'At the Golden Pear' is frequented as much by locals and visiting dignitaries as it is by tourists. In summer you can opt for a table in its leafy *zahradní restaurace* (garden restaurant) across the street. (📞220 514 778; www.restaurantuzlatehrusky.cz; Nový Svět 3; mains 450-590Kč; ⏱11.30am-3pm & 6.30pm-midnight; 🚋22 to Brusnice)

---

### Understand

**Falling Out of Windows**

- - - - - - - - - - - - - - - - - - - - - - - -

Czechs weren't the first to practise 'defenestration' but they've certainly had an unfortunate history of people involuntarily plummeting from windows.

The so-called First Defenestration of Prague was due to religious in-fighting. It occurred in 1419 when Protestants, still angry about the execution of their leader Jan Hus four years earlier, threw several Catholic councillors from Prague's New Town Hall.

The Second Defenestration of Prague in 1618 proved even more devastating. Again, Protestant nobles rebelling against the Catholic Habsburg emperor tossed two councillors and a secretary out of a Prague Castle window (see p25). However, this sectarian act sparked off the Europe-wide Thirty Years' War. It might be pure legend that the defenestrated councillors and secretary lived by falling into the dung-filled moat, but the entire continent most definitely landed in the proverbial.

Besides Jan Masaryk's 1948 defenestration from Černin Palace, other instances include that of novelist Bohumil Hrabal (see p84). In a surreal twist befitting one of his own stories, Hrabal died in 1997 when he fell from a 5th-floor hospital window while feeding pigeons.

## Local Life
### Josef Pleskot's Tunnel

Architect Josef Pleskot's arty 2002 **tunnel** (⏱Apr-Oct; 🚊22, 23 to Pražský hrad) – red-brick and rather Freudian in theme – beneath the castle's Powder Bridge makes a quirky alternative castle exit. Turn west from the bridge's castle side and follow the footpath down into the moat to reach it. If you keep going, you'll reach Malostranská metro.

### Bellavista

ITALIAN €€

9 🍴 Map p34, A4

Several restaurants in and around the Strahov Monastery are aimed at overseas visitors. This, however, boasts a terrace with amazing views, and is upmarket enough to have served the Rolling Stones and Sean Connery. (📞220 517 274; www.kolkovna.cz; Strahovské nádvoří 1; mains 185-295Kč; 23 to Pohořelec; 📶)

### Malý Buddha

ASIAN €

10 🍴 Map p34, A3

Candlelight, incense and a Buddhist shrine characterise this cosy, vaulted restaurant, which hints at an Eastern tearoom. The menu boasts Thai, Chinese and – unusually for Prague – Vietnamese dishes, many of them vegetarian. Drinks include ginseng wine, coconut and mango juices and nearly 40 kinds of tea. (www.malybuddha.cz; Úvoz 46; mains 120-250Kč; ⏱closed Mon; 🚊22 to Pohořelec; 🖋)

# Drinking

### U Černého vola

PUB

11 🍺 Map p34, B3

Being the sort of bar where locals stare at new faces (ie yours), the wonderful 'Black Ox' has managed to maintain an authentic atmosphere

## Understand
### Curse of the Czech Crown Jewels

In St Vitus Cathedral, on the southern side of the Chapel of St Wenceslas (p31), there's a small door locked with seven keys. In a nod to the seven seals of Revelations, each is in the safekeeping of a separate official.

What lies beyond this secretive and carefully guarded door? The Czech crown jewels, of course. They're rarely exhibited to the public, but the oldest among them is the 22-carat-gold St Wenceslas Crown, made for Charles IV in 1347 and dedicated to the earlier prince.

Like all the best regal artefacts, the crown comes with a legendary curse; any usurper wearing it is doomed to die within the year. Call it coincidence, but the Nazi chief in Prague, Reinhard Heydrich, donned the crown in 1941 and was duly assassinated in 1942 by the resistance (see p105).

while remaining right on a tourist strip. The long tables, coats of arms and drinkers staring into their delicious Kozel beer make it feel ancient; in fact, it was built after WWII. The major pity is that it closes so early. (Loretánské náměstí 1; ⏲10am-10pm; 🚃22 to Pohořelec)

### U Zavěšenýho Kafe
BAR

**12** 🚃 Map p34, C3

The 'Hanging Coffee Cup' is named after the charming old practice of buying an extra mug on the off chance a poor fellow customer might need it, and there's certainly a collegiate feel in this legendary superb drinking den. The cosy wood-panelled back room, with its weird art and '60s jukebox, is the best spot to enjoy the beer, coffee and pub grub offered. (www.uzavesenyhokafe.com; Úvoz 6; 🚃22 to Pohořelec)

# Shopping

### Rocking Horse Toy Shop
TOYS

**13** 🔒 Map p34, A3

A cut above, this wonderful shop is palpably a labour of love for discerning owner Ivan Karhan, who's assembled high-quality wooden carved folk dolls, old 1950s wind-up steel tractors, toy cars and even a few rocking

**Understand**

## Good King Wenceslas Looked Out...

English clergyman John Mason Neale wrote the Christmas carol 'Good King Wenceslas' in 1853, inspired by the tale of a page and his master taking food and firewood to the poor on a freezing Boxing Day. However, Neale was either mistaken or exaggerated. Wenceslas (Václav in Czech) wasn't a king, but the duke of Bohemia.

In that capacity, from 925 to 929, Wenceslas helped bring Christianity to Czech lands. Now Czechs' chief patron saint, his image pops up across town, from St Vitus Cathedral to the Wenceslas Statue.

Despite his piety, however, Wenceslas came to an unfortunate end, murdered by his brother Boleslav for cosying up to neighbouring Germans.

horses. For a typically Czech souvenir, the famous and ubiquitous Little Mole character is here in several guises, but this small store also stocks quality toys and art supplies you won't find elsewhere in the city. (Hračky – houpací kůň; Loretánské náměstí 3; 🚃22 to Pohořelec)

Explore

# Petřín Hill
# & Malá Strana

At the foot of Petřín Hill, Malá Strana comprises a picturesque network of winding cobblestone streets and colourful buildings. The one-time market town was destroyed in the Great Fire of 1541, then given a baroque makeover. By the 18th century it was a bohemian quarter befitting its 'left bank' position – and it became the temporary home of Mozart and Casanova.

RICHARD NEBESKY/LONELY PLANET IMAGES ©

# The Sights in a Day

After having a breakfast fit for kings at **Café Savoy** (p49), walk through the grand **Wallenstein Garden** (p44), then stop to see the Infant of Prague at the **Church of Our Lady Victorious** (p47). Catch a glimpse of the moving **Memorial to the Victims of Communism** (p43) monument before boarding the **Petřín Funicular** to the top of **Petřín Hill** (p42). If it's a clear day, ascend the **Lookout Tower** for sweeping views over the city's red rooftops.

Consider having lunch in the park, again with amazing views, at **Restaurant Nebozízek** (p51). Continue hiking downhill until you reach Malá Strana again. Head to the **Franz Kafka Museum** (p47), stopping afterwards for a glass of Moravian wine at **Vinograf** (p52) or to browse Czech titles at **Shakespeare & Sons** (p54). Continue your stroll towards **Kampa Island** (p45).

Enjoy sunset on the riverside. Stop for a break at **Cafe Bar Páty přes Devátý** (p45), overlooking the scenic Čertovka (Devil's Stream), or continue on to local favourite **Mill Kavárna** (p45). Look back towards Prague Castle for dazzling views of the illuminated cathedral and palaces.

For a local's day in Petřín Hill & Malá Strana, see p44.

 **Top Sights**

Petřín Hill (p42)

**Local Life**

Gardens of Malá Strana (p44)

**Best of Prague**

**Bars & Pubs**
Baráčnická rychta (p52)

Zanzibar (p52)

Vinograf (p52)

**Food**
Café Savoy (p49)

Kampa Park (p50)

Pálffy Palác (p50)

**Museums**
Franz Kafka Museum (p47)

**Culture**
U Malého Glena (p54)

## Getting There

🚋 **Tram** Take tram 22 to Újezd or Pohořelec.

Ⓜ **Metro** The closest stop is Malostranská on Line A.

## Top Sights
# Petřín Hill

This hilly, forested city playground was immortalised in Milan Kundera's books. Most attractions atop this lookout point were built in the late 19th to early 20th centuries, creating a slightly innocent, fun-fair atmosphere. The huge stone fortifications that run from Újezd to Strahov, cutting across Petřín's peak, are more sobering – the Hunger Wall, built in 1362 under Charles IV, was constructed by the city's poor in return for food under an early job-creation scheme.

◉ Map p46, A4

admission to park free

⊘ Lookout Tower from 10am, closing times vary; observatory opening times vary; funicular 9am-11pm

Ⓜ Malostranská

Funicular to Petřín Hill

# Don't Miss

### Petřín Funicular

While you can walk up Petřín along several routes – from Hradčany via Strahov or directly from Újezd – by far the most fun way to arrive is on this funicular railway from Újezd. Services leave every 15 to 20 minutes. Ordinary public transport tickets are valid and drivers always seem keen to help if you need it.

### Petřín Lookout Tower

Most long-time residents say the best views of Prague are from the top of this 62m-tall Eiffel Tower lookalike. It's certainly impressive to see the Central Bohemia forests on a clear day from the **Lookout Tower** (50Kč). The tower, which has 299 steps, was built in 1891 for the Prague Exposition.

### Memorial to the Victims of Communism

At the foot of Petřín Hill is this striking sculpture by Olbram Zoubek featuring male figures – in various stages of desiccation – descending a concrete staircase. Through the centre of the steps, a metal line counts the victims: 327 shot while trying to flee across the border, 170,938 driven into exile, 205,486 arrested, 248 executed and 4500 who died in prison.

### Petřín (Štefanik) Observatory

This 1920s **'people's observatory'** (adult/concession 65/45Kč), which boasts a double Zeiss astrograph telescope for observation of the sun or the night sky, is open for public daytime and night-time observations in fair weather. Its odd hours (check the website, www.observatory.cz) mean you have to plan ahead if you want to visit.

## ☑ Top Tips

▶ Stop at one of Malá Strana's bakeries or supermarkets to pick up picnic fixings, then head for a quiet bench in the park to enjoy lunch with a view.

▶ If you're in the mood for some physical exercise, hiking up Petřín Hill is pleasant (and fairly easy if you follow the park's winding paths).

▶ Take the funicular to the top of the hill at night for glittering views over the city.

▶ From Prague Castle, wandering downhill along the paths of Petřín Hill is a delightful way to continue onto Malá Strana.

## ✖ Take a Break

Touristy but fun, Restaurant Nebozízek (p51) is located halfway up Petřín Hill's funicular route – it offers wonderful views and is also accessible by foot.

At the foot of Petřín Hill, try Artisan Restaurant & Cafe (p51) for coffee or the lunch special.

# Local Life
# Gardens of Malá Strana

The aristocrats who inhabited 18th-century Malá Strana created beautiful gardens, many of which are now open to the public. Today, when the sun shines, the neighbourhood's parks and gardens fill up with local students toting their sketchbooks, young mothers and children, and businessmen relaxing on their lunch breaks. Between April and October, everything is in bloom.

......................................................

**1** Admire Wallenstein Garden

One of Prague's tucked-away treasures, Wallenstein Garden is a hidden green world of formal lawns, fountains, ponds and statues. There are entrances via the Wallenstein Palace and from Letenská, but for that true through-the-looking-glass experience, take the gate

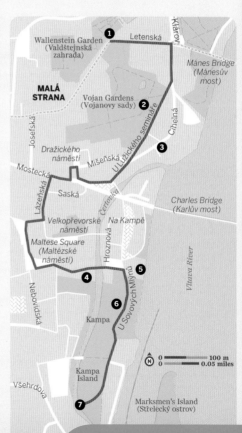

beside Malostranská metro station. Turn left from the escalators and then right on the steps.

**❷ Hang Out with Locals in Vojan Gardens**
While less manicured than most of Malá Strana's parks, Vojan Gardens is a popular spot with locals who like to come here to take a breather with the kids, sit in the sun, or even hold summer parties.

**❸ Spot an Unusual Fountain**
In the open-air plaza in front of the Franz Kafka Museum is a much-photographed public artwork: David Černý's sculpture **Piss** (Proudy; Cihelná). The quirky animatronic sculpture features two guys relieving themselves into a puddle shaped like the Czech Republic. The microchip-controlled sculptures write out famous Prague literary quotations.

**❹ Have a Drink by the Devil's Stream**
Just try to find a prettier alfresco spot for a cup of coffee – or a glass of chilled Moravian white wine – than **Cafe Bar Pátý přes Devátý** (www.59cafebar.cz; Nosticova 8; ◷11am-11pm) The patio's picnic tables look over the quiet Čertovka (Devil's Stream) and the adorable bridge that crosses it to reach Kampa Island.

**❺ Head for Kampa Island**
Cross the little bridge over the Čertovka onto Kampa Island. To the left, note the metal plaques marking the level of the terrible 1890 and 2002 floods in Prague. For more, see p48.

**❻ Feel the Breeze at Kampa**
Toss a Frisbee, take a load off, or just watch the local hipsters play with their dogs at the leafy riverside park known simply as Kampa (from the Latin *campus* or 'field'). One of the city's favourite chill-out zones, it's usually littered with lounging bodies – and excessively romantic teenagers – in summer.

**❼ Hear Music at the Mill**
**Mill Kavárna** (Kampa Park; ◷noon-midnight), an artists' cafe-bar in Kampa Park, has existed in various guises since the communist era. A few tourists are starting to find their way over the wooden footbridge beside the wooden mill wheel, but mainly it's local alternative types who fill the smoky, dimly lit interior, arriving for coffee, beer and the occasional live gig.

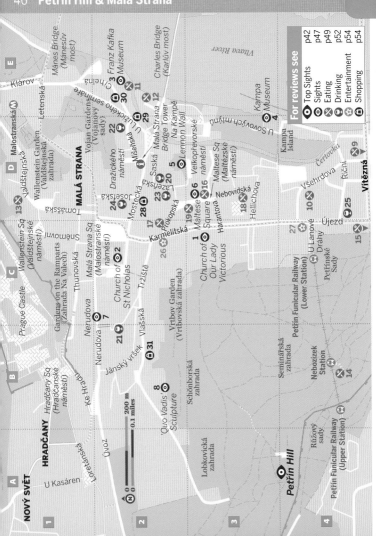

Mánes Bridge (Mánesův most)

Klárov

Letenská

Malostranská Ⓜ

Ⓓ Valdštejnská

Prague Castle

Hradčany Sq (Hradčanské náměstí)

HRADČANY

NOVÝ SVĚT

U Kasáren

Lobkovická zahrada

Loretánská

Úvoz

Ke Hra

Nerudova

Thunovská

Snêmovní

Tomášská

Wallenstein Sq (Valdštejnské náměstí)

13 Ⓓ

Wallenstein Garden (Valdštejnská zahrada)

Gardens on the Ramparts (Zahrada Na Valech)

Ⓒ 7 Church of St Nicholas

Malá Strana Sq (Malostranské náměstí)

2 Ⓒ

Tržiště

Nerudova

Jánský vršek

21 Ⓒ

31 Ⓒ

Vlašská

Schönborská zahrada

8 Ⓒ Quo Vadis? Sculpture

Vrtbov Garden (Vrtbovská zahrada)

Karmelitská

26 Ⓒ

1 Ⓒ Church of Our Lady Victorious

Petřín Hill

Růžový sady

Petřín Funicular Railway (Upper Station)

200 m
0.1 miles

3 Franz Kafka Museum

U Lužického semináře

Vojan Garden (Vojanovy sady)

22 Ⓓ

Dražického náměstí

Saská Malá Strana Bridge Tower

Na Kampě

Misenská

Josefská

24 Ⓓ

Mostecká

Lázeňská

23 Ⓓ 20 Ⓓ

28 Ⓓ

17 Prokopská

5 Ⓓ

Lennon Wall

30 Ⓓ 29 Ⓓ

11 Ⓔ

12 Ⓔ

Charles Bridge (Karlův most)

Kampa Museum 4 Ⓓ

U Sovových mlýnů

Kampa Island

Čertovku

Vltava River

19 Ⓓ

Maltese 6 Ⓓ Square 16 Ⓓ

Nebovidská

Maltese Sq (Maltézské náměstí)

Velkopřevorské náměstí

Harantová

18 Ⓓ

Hellichova

10 Ⓓ

Všehrdova

Říční

9 Ⓔ

Vítězná

27 Ⓒ

U Lanové Dráhy

Petřínské Sady

25 Ⓒ

Újezd

15 Ⓒ

Semínářská zahrada

Nebozízek Station

14 Ⓒ

Petřín Funicular Railway (Lower Station)

**For reviews see**

Ⓒ Top Sights    p42
Ⓒ Sights         p47
Ⓒ Eating         p49
Ⓒ Drinking       p52
Ⓒ Entertainment  p54
Ⓒ Shopping       p54

# Sights

## Church of Our Lady Victorious   CHURCH

1  Map p46, C3

This church contains an important relic: the 400-year-old 'Infant of Prague', said to have protected the city for centuries. The tradition of dressing the 47cm-tall wax figure from a wardrobe of 70 costumes continues today, with nuns changing his robes according to a religious calendar. (Look for mentions of the 'Bambino di Praga' in the classic Czech novel *I served the King of England*.) (Kostel Panny Marie Vítězné; www.pragjesu.info; Karmelitská 9; admission by donation; ☉8.30am-7pm Mon-Sat, to 8pm Sun, closed 25 Dec & Easter Mon; ☐12, 22 to Hellichova)

## Church of St Nicholas   CHURCH

2  Map p46, C2

Malá Strana is dominated by the huge green cupola of Prague's finest baroque building. Begun by famous Bavarian architect Kristof Dientzenhofer and continued by his son Kilian, the church boasts Europe's largest fresco, Johann Kracker's 1770 *Apotheosis of St Nicholas,* on its ceiling. (www.psalterium.cz; adult/child 70/35Kč, admission to tower adult/child 70/50Kč; ☉9am-5pm Mar-Oct, to 4pm Nov-Feb; ☐12, 20, 22 to Malostranské náměstí)

## Franz Kafka Museum   MUSEUM

3  Map p46, E2

Don't be deterred by the Oedipus-complex talk at the start of this contemporary museum. Just enjoy the trippy movie about Prague, the exhibits that curve through translucent netting, the rows of filing cabinets, a claustrophobic, strobe-lit section and original documents and photos. Although some call it pretentious (and it's more fulfilling for speakers of Kafka's native German), it's essential for serious fans. (Muzeum Franzy Kafky; www.kafkamuseum.cz; Cihelná 2b; adult/child 180/120Kč; ☉10am-6pm; Ⓜ Malostranská)

## Kampa Museum   MUSEUM

4  Map p46, D3

Its prime location on the Vltava's left bank makes this flour-mill-turned-gallery as attractive as the work it contains. So while acquainting yourself with Otto Gutfreund's cubist sculptures, František Kupka paintings and other modern Central European art, don't forget to enjoy the roof terrace facing Petřín Hill. The huge wooden chair on the wall in the river is best viewed through the small concave mirror in one of the galleries or from the riverside terrace cafe in summer. (Muzeum Kampa; www.museumkampa.cz; U Sovových mlýnů 2; adult/concession permanent collection 160/80Kč, special exhibits 90/45Kč; ☉10am-6pm; ☐9, 12, 20, 22 to Újezd)

### Lennon Wall
HISTORIC SITE

5  Map p46, D2

Dissidents in communist Czechoslovakia often revered Western rock musicians like John Lennon for flouting social norms. And after Lennon's 1980 murder this wall was painted with his image and turned into a graffiti splattered memorial – repainted each time the secret police whitewashed over it. Today, though the wall looks like any other graffiti-splattered monument, it remains a symbol of youthful yearning for free speech and peace during a time of political oppression. (Velkopřevorské náměstí; ⊟12, 20, 22 to Malostranské náměstí)

### Maltese Square
HISTORIC SITE

6  Map p46, D3

References to the Knights of Malta around Malá Strana hark back to 1169, when that military order established a

### Local Life
**Kampa Island**

A lovely little green oasis, Kampa Island (Map p46, D4) is separated from Malá Strana proper by a canal known as the Devil's Stream (Čertovka). Two mill wheels survive, where washerwomen used to do laundry until the 1930s. Nowadays, the island attracts young families, dog-walkers and artists. Night-time views of the lights twinkling across the river are superb, particularly from the south of the island. Take tram 6, 9, 12, 20, or 22 to Újezd.

monastery in the Church of Our Lady Beneath the Chain on this square. Disbanded by the communists, the Knights have regained much property under post-1989 restitution laws, including the Lennon Wall. (Maltézské náměstí; ⊟12, 20, 22 to Malostranské náměstí)

### Nerudova
STREET

7  Map p46, C2

Malá Strana's main thoroughfare plunges steeply downhill from the castle to Malostranské náměstí. Today it's lined with touristy restaurants and shops, but you can still admire the 'baroque-ified' Renaissance facades and ornate old house signs (see the boxed text, p51). Casanova and Mozart shared lodgings in 1791 at No 33, Bretfeldský Palace. Czech writer Jan Neruda, after whom the street takes its current name, lived at No 47, At the Two Suns (1845–57). (⊟12, 20, 22 to Malostranské náměstí)

### Quo Vadis Sculpture
SCULPTURE

8  Map p46, B2

Not strictly a public monument, this golden Trabant car on four legs is a David Černý tribute to 4000 East Germans who occupied the garden of the then West German Embassy in 1989, before being granted political asylum and leaving their Trabants behind. Today's German embassy is happy for you to peer through its back fence at the sculpture. (Behind the German Embassy, Vlašská 19; ⊟12, 20, 22, 23 to Malostranské náměstí)

DOUG MCKINLAY/LONELY PLANET IMAGES ©

Kampa Museum (p47)

# Eating

## Café Savoy
CAFE €€

9  Map p46, D4

This gorgeous coffeehouse is one of Prague's best. Come for the stunning interior, brilliant breakfasts, Czech and French specialities, tasty coffees and good winelist. Local critics say it's a slice of culinary life from Czechoslovakia's First Republic days (1918–38). Evening bookings are recommended. (☎257 311 562; www.ambi.cz; Vítězná 5; mains 225-298Kč; 🚋6, 9, 12, 20, 22 to Újezd; 😊)

## Bar Bar
INTERNATIONAL €

10  Map p46, D4

This cosy, friendly cellar bar has a bohemian feel with its mix of antiques and contemporary arty touches, plus one of the most interesting menus in town. Delicious food runs the gamut from homemade Italian risotto and French crêpes to Norwegian salmon. (www.bar-bar.cz; Všehrdova 17; mains 145-295Kč; 🚋6, 9, 12, 20, 22 to Újezd; 🖉)

## Hergetova Cihelná
INTERNATIONAL €€€

11  Map p46, E2

Slightly less starry and more affordable than its sister, Kampa Park, this converted 18th-century *cihelná* (brickworks) is rated as a better bet by many locals, despite some grumbles about the consistency of its food. Hergetova Cihelná also boasts fantastic riverside views and a menu including pasta, fish, meat, Czech specialities and seasonal Asian dishes. (☏ 257 535 534; www.kampagroup.com; Cihelná 2b; mains 395-495Kč; M Malostranská; ☜)

you overlook the lights of Charles Bridge. (☏ 257 532 685; www.kampagroup .com; Na Kampě 8b; mains 485-895Kč; ☒ 12, 20, 22 to Malostranské náměstí; ☜ ✐)

## Kampa Park INTERNATIONAL €€€

12 ☒ Map p46, E2

At Prague's most famous restaurant, a celebrity magnet since 1994, Mick Jagger, Johnny Depp, Lauren Bacall, Robbie Williams and Bill and Hillary Clinton have all overtipped the staff; ordinary mortals come for a special evening. The modern international cuisine runs from spinach soufflé to Norwegian salmon with vanilla mash. However, the location is truly stunning: from the riverside cobblestone terrace

## Pálffy Palác FRENCH, INTERNATIONAL €€€

13 ☒ Map p46, D1

Dining by candlelight among the dining room's faded grandeur or overlooking the palace gardens from the 1st-floor terrace is a memorable experience. In the same neo-baroque palace as the Prague Conservatoire, the Pálffy is popular for set weekday lunches with nearby embassy and government office staff. Now with a Sunday brunch buffet. (www.palffy.cz; Valdštejnská 14; set lunch 290-390Kč, mains 390-590Kč; M Malostranská)

Wallenstein Garden (p44)

Understand

## The Numbers Game

Until numbering was introduced in the 18th century, exotic house names and signs were the only way of identifying individual Prague buildings. This practice came to a halt in 1770 when it was banned by the city fathers.

More such-named houses and signs survive in Nerudova (p48) than along any other Prague street. As you head downhill look out for At the Two Suns (No 47), the Golden Horseshoe (No 34), the Three Fiddles (No 12), the Red Eagle (No 6) and the Devil (No 4). Other signs include a St Wenceslas on horseback (No 34), a golden key (No 27) and a golden goblet (No 16).

## Restaurant Nebozízek
INTERNATIONAL €€

14  Map p46, B4

This 17th-century conservatory restaurant halfway up Petřín Hill now has a designer interior, with lots of pale Nordic furniture and Singapore orchids, as well as a menu that peppers its modern international menu with a few Czech staples. The views are fabulous, even if the place feels touristy. (www.nebozizek.cz; Petřínské sady 411; mains 150-420Kč; 🚋6, 9, 12, 20, 22 to Újezd, then Petřín funicular)

## Artisan Restaurant & Cafe
CAFE €

15  Map p46, C4

This new cafe-style eatery wins points for its shaded garden with outdoor tables, homemade bread and pasta, and lunch specials like pumpkin risotto and vegetarian moussaka. As an added bonus, the place is strictly nonsmoking. (www.artisanrestaurant.cz; Rošických 603/4; mains 195-325Kč; 🚋6, 9, 12, 20, 22 to Újezd; ❷ 🛜 🍴)

## U Malé Velryby
INTERNATIONAL €€

16  Map p46, D3

At this cosy backstreet eatery (translation: 'Little Whale'), the friendly chef-owner from Ireland creates tasty seafood plates. Try the crab pasta or calamari *ceviche,* or settle in with a few tapas and a good bottle of wine. (www.umalevelryby.cz; Maltézské náměstí 15; mains 310-350Kč; ⏱noon-3pm & 6-11pm; 🚋12, 20, 22, 23 to Malostranské náměstí)

## U Maltézských Rytířů
CZECH, INTERNATIONAL €€€

17  Map p46, C2

'At the Knights of Malta' is a romantic restaurant, serving top-notch and determinedly old-fashioned Czech cuisine like roast wild boar with rose-hip sauce and duck breast in walnut sauce at candlelit tables under Gothic arches. Don't miss the owner's legendary strudel – and book well ahead. (☎257 530 075; www.umaltezskychrytiru.com; Prokopská 10; mains 300-890Kč; 🚋12, 20, 22 to Malostranské náměstí)

### U Modré Kachničky

CZECH €€€

18 🍴 Map p46, D3

A baroque hunting lodge hidden away on a quiet side street, 'At the Blue Duckling' is a plush, old-fashioned place with quiet, candlelit nooks perfect for a romantic dinner. The menu is heavy on traditional Bohemian poultry, game and fish dishes. (📞257 320 308; www.umodrekachnicky.cz; Nebovidská 6; mains 475-595Kč; 🚊12, 20, 22 to Hellichova or Újezd)

### Vino Deja Vu

BAR

19 🍴 Map p46, D3

This friendly wine bar and eatery feels surprisingly authentic, given its location right on Maltese Sq. It has outdoor seating so you can watch the people go by as you try the smoked trout salad, baked sandwiches or the homemade pâté with a glass of Czech wine or a seasonal fruit spritzer. (www.vinodejavu.cz; Maltézské náměstí 8; mains 135-155Kč; 🚊6, 9, 12, 20, 22 to Újezd; 🛜)

# Drinking

### Zanzibar

BAR

20 🍺 Map p46, D2

The wait staff could do with the occasional hurry-up, but with over 200 well-priced cocktails and what may be Malá Strana's longest bar, this laneway spot with ancient vaulted ceilings and a thoroughly modern approach to mixology is good for a nightcap after nearby restaurants. (www.zanzi.cz; Lázeňská 65; 🚊12, 20, 22 to Malostranské náměstí)

### Baráčnická Rychta

PUB

21 🍺 Map p46, B2

Atmospherically tucked away behind Nerudova along a winding Malá Strana street, this 19th-century beer hall feels a bit furtive and secretive – at least for this neck of the woods. In the small upstairs bar you can sup four types of Svijanský beer as well as the more common Pilsner Urquell; food is also served. Downstairs, the larger Cabaret Hall hosts big bands and offbeat live gigs. (www.baracnickarychta .cz; Tržiště 23; 🚊12, 20, 22 to Malostranské náměstí, night tram 57)

### Vinograf

BAR

22 🍺 Map p46, D2

This petite wine bar, on a fairly quiet side street, is a fantastic place to sample a few local varietals paired with small plates, cheese and olives. Twenty wines by the glass are available on a rotating basis. Vinograf is conveniently located close to Charles Bridge on the way to the Kafka Museum. (www.vinograf.cz; Míšeňská 8; 🚊12, 20, 22 to Malostranské náměstí; nv)

### Cukrkávalimonáda

CAFE

23 🍺 Map p46, D2

This 20-seat gem is as sweet as its name, 'sugar-coffee-lemonade', which is also the Czech equivalent of 'eeny meeny miny moe'. The floral pattern decorating its historic ceiling beams caps an otherwise fairly bare wooden interior, while the blackboard menu offers delicious pasta, pancakes,

Malá Strana rooftops and Petřín Hill

salads, wines and cakes. The 'superior' hot chocolate of 70% melted dark chocolate is positively primordial; apparently some even manage to finish it. (www.cukrkavalimonada.com; Lázeňská 7; ⏱9am-7pm; 🚋12, 20, 22 to Malostranské náměstí; 😊🍴)

## Blue Light
BAR

**24** 🚇 Map p46, D2

The Blue Light is an appropriately dark and atmospheric jazz cavern where you can enjoy a relaxed cocktail as you cast your eye over the vintage posters, records and graffiti that adorn the walls. Although the background jazz is recorded rather than live, it's played on a quality sound system that never overpowers your conversation. (www.bluelightbar.cz; Josefská 1; 🚋12, 20, 22 to Malostranské náměstí, night tram 57)

## Klub Újezd
CLUB

**25** 🚇 Map p46, D4

As interesting to visit as it is to pronounce after a few beers, Klub Újezd (u-yez-d) is one of Prague's many 'alternative' bars, filled with a fascinating collection of handmade furniture and fittings, original art and weird wrought-iron sculptures. The three-floor venue progresses from a cellar DJ bar to a ground-floor pub and an upstairs cafe. (www.klubujezd.cz; Újezd 18; 🚋6, 9, 12, 20, 22 to Újezd, night tram 57, 58, 59)

# Entertainment

### U Malého Glena
BAR, CLUB

26 ⭐ Map p46, C2

'Little Glen's' really is little, so get here early. Yet the intimate size makes this US-owned jazz-blues venue-restaurant so vital. Performers like Stan the Man put their heart and soul into entertaining an audience mere centimetres away. Add cocktails and you've got a memorable night out. (www.malyglen.cz; Karmelitská 23; ⏰music from 9.30pm; 🚋12, 20, 22 to Malostranské náměstí, night tram 57)

### Popocafepetl Music Club
CLUB

27 ⭐ Map p46, C4

The latest branch of the popular mini-chain is a small club and live-music venue promising a deliberately eclectic mix: blues, Balkan, drum and bass, ska, punk and more. (www.popocafepetl. cz; Újezd 19; ⏰bands from 8.30pm; 🚋6, 9, 12, 20, 22 to Újezd, night tram 57, 58, 59)

# Shopping

### Manufaktura
ARTS & CRAFTS

28 🔒 Map p46, D2

There are several Manufaktura outlets across town, but this small branch right near Charles Bridge seems to keep its trim inventory especially enticing. You'll find great Czech wooden toys, beautiful-looking (if extremely chewy) honey gingerbread made from elaborate medieval moulds, and seasonal gifts such as charming hand-painted Easter eggs. A zingy new line is its range of beer-infused cosmetics. (www.manufaktura.cz; Mostecká 17; Ⓜ Malostranská, 🚋12, 20, 22 to Malostranské náměstí)

### Shakespeare & Sons
BOOKS

29 🔒 Map p46, D2

This small but classic city bookshop is filled with English-language titles both old and new. It's a fine place to browse titles by Kundera, Kafka

---

### Understand

### Kafka's Neighbourhood

'Someone must have been telling lies about Josef K, for without having done anything wrong, he was arrested one fine morning' – that opening line to Franz Kafka's *The Trial* (1925) is widely considered among the greatest in world literature. The words are also a testament to Prague's disorientating nature; and in the writer's home city it's hard not to be moved by his genius. Of course, it's simple to pay tribute to Kafka by visiting his birthplace (p78) or grave. But true fans will want to use the opportunity to delve more into the novelist's complex relationship with Prague, which he complained was small and claustrophobic but got under your skin. The Franz Kafka Museum (p47) is just the place.

and other translated works by Czech literary heavyweights. (www.shakes.cz; U Lužického semináře 10; Ⓜ Malostranská, 🚃 12, 20, 22 to Malostranské náměstí)

## Franz Kafka Museum Store

BOOKS

**30** 🔒 Map p46, E2

As Prague's tourist-oriented shops go, the museum store at the Franz Kafka Museum is pretty classy: you won't see cheap coloured glass or tacky plastic beer mugs here, just an elegant assortment of postcards, books, prints, stationery and small gifts related to Kafka, Mucha and the city itself. (www .kafkamuseum.cz; Cihelná 2b; ⊙ 10am-6pm; Ⓜ Malostranská)

## Pavla & Olga

FASHION

**31** 🔒 Map p46, B2

Quirky-yet-fashionable clothes and hats are the handiwork of sisters Pavla and Olga Michalková, who originally were costume designers in the film and TV industry. Past customers include photographer Helmut Newton, Britpop band Blur and Czech supermodel Tereza Maxová, although the unique and idiosyncratic designs are still suitable for slightly lesser names like yourself. (www.fashion-gallery .cz; Vlašská 13; 🚃 12, 20, 22 to Malostranské náměstí)

## Local Life
# Alternative Art in Smíchov

Standing in contrast to the fairy-tale historic sphere of castles and royal gardens, working-class Smíchov is an industrial district on the Vltava's left bank. With its vibrant contemporary art scene and unpretentious bars, the slightly gritty neighbourhood offers an authentic taste of Czech life; its character is slowly changing with the construction of contemporary buildings and the influx of new businesses.

### Getting There

**M** **Metro** Line B to Anděl

**🚊 Tram** Lines 4, 7, 10, 14, 16 run through Smíchov to stops Bertramka and Anděl

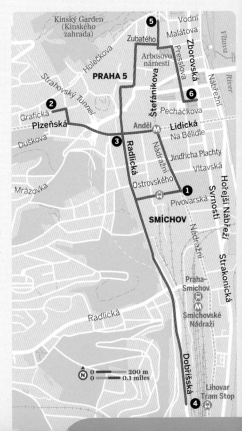

**❶ Beer at the Original Staropramen Brewery**

To soak up some of Smíchov's down-to-earth charm – and feel the gentrification that's currently under-way – pull up a barstool at **Potrefena Husá Na Verandách** (Staropramen Brewery; www.phnaverandach.cz; Nádražní 84), housed in the neighbourhood's original Staropramen Brewery. Beer has been brewed here since 1871. Today the place is classy, but the brews are the same; in summer, sit outside on the terrace.

**❷ Modern Art at Futura**

Home to *Brown-nosing* (2003) by David Černý, the **Futura Centre for Contemporary Art** (www.futuraproject .cz; Holečkova 49; admission free; 11am-6pm Wed-Sun) lets you stick your head inside the bum of a huge, bent-over statue. The slick three-floor gallery space hosts rotating modern art exhibits.

**❸ Czech Food at Zlaty Klas**

Cosy *tankovna* restaurant **Zlaty Klas** (www.zlatyklas.cz; Plzeňská 9; mains 150-195Kč) is well loved among locals for its hearty, well-prepared Czech cuisine – try the killer baked pork ribs – plus beers on tap and a long list of wine and mixed drinks.

**❹ Cultural Events at the MeetFactory**

For cutting-edge film screenings, concerts, theatrical performances, lectures and art installations, find out what's happening at David Černý's **MeetFactory** (251 551 796; www.meet factory.cz; Ke Sklárně 3213/15; hours vary by event), a multifaceted gallery, exhibition space and entertainment venue. Look for the giant red cars – and be careful crossing the railway tracks.

**❺ Avant-Garde Theatre at Švandovo divadlo**

The funky theatre and nightspot **Švandovo divadlo** (234 651 111; www.svandovodivadlo.cz; Štefánikova 57; ticket prices vary; 6, 9, 12, 20 to Švandovo Divadlo) stages avant-garde theatre and acoustic music performances; the place also hosts art exhibits and events. Check online for full listings of what's going on.

**❻ Dancing at Futurum**

The sister venue of Lucerna Music Bar, **Futurum** (www.futurum.musicbar.cz; Zborovská 7; cover 100Kč; 9pm-3.30am Fri & Sat; 4, 7, 10, 14 to Zborovská, night tram 54, 57, 58, 59 from Anděl) also does lively '80s and '90s parties with music videos projected on a huge screen above the dance floor.

Explore

# Jewish Museum & Josefov

The lovely Josefov is the site of the former Jewish ghetto – a place where the city's large Jewish population used to be locked in at night. Today, their synagogues and cemetery form the popular Jewish Museum. Though the cobblestoned streets are alive with cool cocktail bars and Czech pubs, one still feels an eerie quiet here sometimes that evokes the neighbourhood's past.

*SHAUN HIGSON COLOUR / ALAMY ©*

# The Sights in a Day

Arrive at the **Jewish Museum** (p60) first thing in the morning, heading first for the big-ticket attraction – the **Jewish Cemetery** (pictured left; p62) – the place is much more atmospheric when you're not with a huge crowd. Stop into the **Maisel Synagogue** and the **Pinkas Synagogue**, then take a well-deserved coffee break at **Bakeshop Praha** (p65) – and treat yourself to a chocolate croissant while you're at it. Properly caffeinated? Move on to a mini-tour of the beautiful **Spanish Synagogue**.

If you haven't had enough Jewish history yet, hit the **Old-New Synagogue** (p65) and the **Jewish Town Hall** (p65). Stop for a late lunch – including a beer, of course – at classy corner pub **Kolkovna** (p66). You'll be nearby the **Franz Kafka Monument** (p65), which is fun for a quick look (and a photo op).

Time for a little night music: choose from a classical concert at the riverside **Rudolfinum** (p67) or opt for an edgier evening with live music at hollowed-out one-time theatre the **Roxy** (p69). Before or after the show, stop into **Tretter's New York Bar** (p66) for an expertly prepared martini.

## Top Sights

Jewish Museum (p60)

Jewish Cemetery (p62)

## Best of Prague

**Bars & Pubs**

Kolkovna (p66)

U Rudolfina (p66)

Tretter's New York Bar (p66)

Pivovarský Klub (p67)

**Food**

Bakeshop Praha (p65)

**Shopping**

Kotva (p69)

Granát Turnov (p69)

**Nightlife**

M1 Lounge (p66)

Roxy (p69)

**History**

Old-New Synagogue (p65)

Spanish Synagogue (p61)

## Getting There

Ⓜ **Metro** Line A to Staroměstská.

Ⓜ **Metro** Line B to Namestí Republiky.

## Top Sights
# Jewish Museum

Prague's Jewish Town, like other former Jewish ghettos across Europe, has seen some tough times. This museum was first established in 1906 to preserve artefacts from the neighbourhood's synagogues, was closed during WWII, and remained largely defunct for decades before the museum was restored to the Jewish community in 1994 after the fall of communism. Today it comprises six important Jewish sites; according to the Czech Tourist Authority, this museum was the city's most visited in 2010.

Map p64, B3

bookings 222 317 191

www.jewishmuseum.cz

U Staré školy 1

admission all sites adult/concession 300/200Kč

9am-6pm Sun-Fri Apr-Oct, to 4.30pm Nov-Mar

M Staroměstská

Spanish Synagogue

# Don't Miss

### Klaus Synagogue & Ceremonial Hall
Both the baroque Klaus Synagogue and the nearby Ceremonial Hall contain exhibits on Jewish ceremonies and other traditions, most interesting for the historian or devout visitor. (Klauzová synagóga & Obřadní Síň; U Starého hřbitova 1)

### Maisel Synagogue
Mordechai Maisel was mayor of the Jewish ghetto under the liberal rule of Emperor Rudolf II during the 16th and 17th centuries. He was also the richest man in the city of Prague; in addition to various public works, he paid for this synagogue to be built for his private use. Today, the space houses rotating exhibitions. (Maiselova synagóga; Maiselova 10)

### Pinkas Synagogue
Built in 1535, this was used for worship until 1941. Today it's a moving Holocaust memorial, its walls inscribed with the names, birth dates and dates of disappearance of 77,297 Czech Jews. (Pinkasova synagóga; Široká 3)

### Spanish Synagogue
The most beautiful of the museum's synagogues, this boasts an ornate Moorish interior, an exhibition on recent Jewish history and a handy bookshop. (Španělská synagóga; Vězeňská 1)

## ☑ Top Tips

▶ Note that the museum is always closed on Saturday (Sabbath).

▶ Ticket options are complicated: most visitors are best off purchasing the ticket allowing access to all museum sites.

▶ Men must cover their heads. Yarmulkes are provided at entrances.

▶ Travellers with a strong interest in Jewish history should consider hiring a private guide, but the museum is also easy to walk through alone.

## ✘ Take a Break

Stop for some of the city's most gourmet coffee and pastries at nearby Bakeshop Praha (p65).

For an excellent pint of beer in the vicinity of the Spanish Synagogue, head to corner pub Kolkovna (p66).

## Top Sights
# Jewish Cemetery

The city authorities once insisted Jews were interred only here – nowhere else – so by the time the 'garden of the dead' stopped taking new burials in 1787 it was full to bursting. Today it holds more than 12,000 tombstones, though as the Jewish Museum points out, many more than that are buried here. Be aware that conditions at this popular attraction sometimes feel almost as crowded for the living as among the dead.

👁 Map p64, A3

📞 reservations 222 317 191

www.jewishmuseum.cz

U Staré školy 1

admission with Jewish Museum ticket

🕙 9am-6pm Sun-Fri Apr-Oct, to 4.30pm Nov-Mar

Ⓜ Staroměstská

Headstones at Jewish Cemetery

# Don't Miss

### Rabbi Loew's Tomb

Sometimes called 'the Jewish hero of the Czechs', Rabbi Judah Loew ben Bezalel was a respected scholar and the chief rabbi of Bohemia in the 16th century. Perhaps more importantly to Czech people, he's part of a legend surrounding the creation of a golem (p67), a figure he supposedly built from clay to protect the Jewish people living in Prague's ghetto.

### Mordechai Maisel's Tomb

This tomb honours a philanthropist with some incredibly deep pockets. In addition to serving as a Jewish leader in the 16th century, Maisel was the city's wealthiest citizen. He paid for the construction of new buildings in the ghetto, had the roads paved, commissioned the Maisel Synagogue (p61) for his own private use and even lent money to Emperor Rudolf II.

### David Gans' Tomb

A noted German historian and astronomer, Gans came to Prague in part to hear the lectures of Rabbi Loew. He's perhaps most famous for his association with Tycho Brahe, who asked Gans to translate the Alphonsine Tables from Hebrew to German.

### Joseph Solomon Delmedigo's Tomb

Another impressive Jewish intellectual represented in the cemetery is Joseph Solomon Delmedigo, both a physician and a philosopher. He studied and worked all over Europe before finally settling in Prague in 1648, where he authored various scientific texts.

## ☑ Top Tips

▶ If you're visiting the Jewish Museum, come first thing in the morning – and head straight for the cemetery, as it tends to get increasingly busy as the day goes on.

▶ Remember that you're in a cemetery – always be careful where you step.

▶ Make a point to see the most famous tombstones, then spend some time looking around the quieter alleys and shadowy corners of the cemetery.

## ✕ Take a Break

After visiting the cemetery, head for happy hour (3pm to 6pm daily), or just a strong coffee, at nearby Casa Blu (p67).

On the river side of the cemetery is U Rudolfina (p66), a down-to-earth local pub ideal for a beer, either pre- or postsightseeing.

0.1 miles
200 m

**JOSEFOV**

**PRAHA 1**

Old-New Synagogue

Jewish Museum

Jewish Cemetery

Franz Kafka Monument

Jewish Town Hall

Čechův most

Vltava River

Old Town Square (Staroměstské náměstí)

Tyn Courtyard (Týnský dvůr)

Jan Palach Square (Náměstí Jana Palacha)

Dvořákovo nábřeží

Dvořákovo nábřeží

U Milosrdných

Bílkova

Dušní

Dušní

Elišky Krásnohorské

Maiselova

Červená

Široká

Kaprova

Valentinská

Křižovnická

Staroměstská

17.listopadu

Pařížská

Jáchymova

Salvátorská

Vězeňská

V Kolkovně

Kozí

Kozí

Rámová

U obecního dvora

Haštalská

Haštalské náměstí

Dlouhá

Rybná

Rybná

Dlouhá

Masná

Týnská

Týnská

Dušní

Malá Štupartská

Jakubská

# Sights

## Jewish Town Hall
HISTORIC SITE

1  Map p64, B3

Next to the Old-New Synagogue, this town hall was built by Jewish ghetto mayor Mordechai Maisel in 1586. It's worth noting for its clock tower, which has one Hebrew face where the hands run 'backwards' like Hebrew script. (Židovská radnice; Ⓜ Staroměstská)

## Old-New Synagogue
SYNAGOGUE

2  Map p64, B3

With its steep roof, Gothic gables and descending entrance, Europe's oldest working synagogue is the source of the most famous golem legend. Dating from the 13th century, it looks much as it would have five centuries ago. The pulpit is surrounded by a wrought-iron grill and on the eastern wall is the Holy Ark holding Torah scrolls. (Staronová synagóga; www.synagogue.cz; Červená 2; Reservation Centre U Starého Hřbitova 3a; adult/child 200/140Kč; ⊙9am-6pm Sun-Fri Apr-Oct, to 4.30pm Sun-Fri Nov-Mar, closed Jewish holidays; Ⓜ Staroměstská)

## Franz Kafka Monument
MONUMENT

3  Map p64, C3

Jaroslav Róna's unusual sculpture of a mini-Franz sitting piggyback on his own headless body was unveiled in 2003. Commissioned by Prague's Franz Kafka Society, it's beside the Spanish Synagogue. (www.franzkafka-soc .cz; Vězeňská; Ⓜ Staroměstská)

# Eating

## Bakeshop Praha
CAFE €

4  Map p64, D3

This isn't just a bakery: this chic but friendly corner spot does an assortment of fresh Mediterranean salads, thick and healthy sandwiches, savoury pies and frothy cappuccinos to take away or eat in. A Josefov classic. (www .bakeshop.cz; Kozí 1; ⊙7am-7pm; mains 85-170Kč; Ⓜ Staroměstská; 🛜 🖉)

## Bodeguita del Medio
CUBAN €€€

5  Map p64, B4

Not far from Old Town Sq, this festive Cuban bar and restaurant and sees nightly crowds gathered around rustic wooden tables in a graffitied, low-lit atmosphere. Flavourful plates include Creole bouillabaisse, prawns with chilli, lime and ginger, or just a classic mojito. (www.labodeguitadelmedio.cz; Kaprova 5; mains 280-485Kč; Ⓜ Staroměstská; 🖉)

## Orange Moon
ASIAN €€

6  Map p64, D3

Buddhist statues, oriental carved-wood panels, paper lanterns and warm, sunny colours make for a welcoming combination at this two-floor popular Asian restaurant. The menu is mostly Thai, with authentically spicy dishes. There are also some Indonesian, Burmese and Indian dishes, with both Singha beer and Pilsner to take the edge off that chilli burn. (www.orangemoon.cz; Rámová 5; mains 195-365Kč; Ⓜ Náměstí Republiky; 🖉)

### Kolkovna
CZECH €€

7 · Map p64, C3

Slightly refined but pleasantly rustic: at the original corner location of Kolkovna's mini-empire the hits keep coming – come here for hearty Czech goulash and potatoes, roast duck and tall, ice-cold beers like Pilsner Urquell and Velkopopovický kozel flowing from polished brass taps. This popular pub brings in locals and tourists alike; last time we visited, there were large groups of local guys meeting here at night, plus a steady stream of curious foreigners. (V Kolkovně 8; www.kolkovna.cz; mains 175-345Kč; M Staroměstská)

### Local Life
### Tankovna Pubs

For drinkers who don't like to stray too far from the source, the Pilsner brewery has been working with pubs and restaurants since 1995 to install large vertical storage tanks in their premises, aiming to keep unpasteurised beer fresh and especially flavoursome (rather than storing it in traditional kegs).

Among the first to serve such *tankovna* beer were the upmarket 'pub reconstructions' Kolkovna and **Celnice** (Map p102, C2; V Celnici 4; ⏱11am-midnight Sun-Thu, to 4am Fri & Sat).

More old-fashioned *tankovna* pubs include U Pinkasů (p96), U Rudolfina (p66) and U Zlatého Tygra (p82).

# Drinking

### Tretter's New York Bar
BAR

8 · Map p64, D3

This sultry 1930s Manhattan-style cocktail bar harks back to gentler times when people went out for nightcaps – and when the drinks were stiff and properly made. Regularly cited as one of the city's top bars, Tretter's brings in the beautiful people and has prices to match. It's on a street with some of the city's best restaurants, so it's a perfect place to stop by after dinner. (www.tretters.cz; V Kolkovně 3; M Staroměstská)

### M1 Lounge
CLUB

9 · Map p64, D3

Prague's most central dance club has a recently expanded dance floor, plush new seating areas and a large cocktail list – standard features. But it's recently rolled out *shisha* menus earlier in the evening (before the dancing gets going) and fresh sushi until 3am. Note that the place is mellow before midnight, then morphs into a full-on dance club through the wee hours. (www.m1lounge.com; Masná 1; admission weekdays free, Fri & Sat 100Kč; ⏱9pm-4am Tue-Fri, 11pm-11am Sat; M Staroměstská)

### U Rudolfina
PUB

10 · Map p64, A4

A rare Old Town *pivnice* that doesn't actively woo tourists, but gets them regardless. Belly up to the downstairs

> ### Understand
> **Golem City**
> ----------------
>
> Tales of golems, or servants created from clay, date back to early Judaism. However, the most famous such mythical creature belonged to 16th-century Prague's Rabbi Loew, of the Old-New Synagogue. Loew is said to have used mud from the Vltava's banks to create a golem to protect the Prague ghetto. However, left alone one Sabbath, the creature ran amok and Rabbi Loew was forced to rush out of a service and remove the magic talisman that kept it moving. He then carried the lifeless body into the synagogue's attic, where some insist it remains. In 1915, Gustav Meyrink's Austrian novel *Der Golem* reprised the story and brought it into the European mainstream.

bar, often filled with Czechs, and have a pint of whatever's on tap. (Křižovnická 10; Ⓜ Staroměstská)

### Casa Blu
BAR

11 Ⓠ Map p64, D2

This Latin American bar feels a little secretive. Inside, street signs in Spanish, Aztec blankets and lots of tequila work together to create a cosy atmosphere for the nightly happy hour (3pm to 6pm). (www.lacasablu.cz; Kozí 15; Ⓜ Staroměstská)

### Kozička
BAR

12 Ⓠ Map p64, D3

The 'Little Goat' rocks in standing-room-only fashion until well after midnight in this buzzing, brick-lined basement bar. Look for the quirky wrought-iron goat sculpture, and descend into good times with a mainly Czech crowd. (www.kozicka.cz; Kozí 1; ⏰ noon-3am; Ⓜ Náměstí Republiky)

### Pivovarský Klub
PUB

13 Ⓠ Map p64, E3

So many beers, so little time. If you're getting a taste for the local *pivo,* head to the Pivovarský Klub. Scores of different bottled brews from around the Czech Republic (and the rest of the world) are on offer, and on tap is a rotating selection of beers from independent breweries around the country. The traditional Czech food is surprisingly good, and the entire pub is nonsmoking. (Křižkova 17; Ⓜ Florenc; )

## Entertainment

### Rudolfinum
CONCERT HALL

14 ⭐ Map p64, A3

Despite a surprisingly small stage, the neo-Renaissance Rudolfinum's main Dvořák Hall has good acoustics and the cachet to attract internationally acclaimed troupes. Home to the Czech

Understand

# Jewish Prague

The story of Prague's Jewish people is a trying one: they've been walled in and persecuted, subjected to extreme poverty and, in many cases, simply eliminated. Given this tumultuous history, it's satisfying to hear the Prague Tourist Authority's recently released statistics – in 2010, the Jewish Museum was the city's most visited museum.

### Early Oppression

Jews began living in Prague in the 9th century, and by the 11th century the city was one of Europe's most important Jewish centres. But the Crusades marked the start of the Jews' plight as the city's oldest synagogue was burned to the ground. By the end of the 12th century, they lost many rights; soon they were forced into a walled ghetto that was locked at night.

Frequently persecuted by the authorities, made to wear special clothing and pushed into servantile positions in the royal chambers, Jews remained third-class citizens through the 13th century while emperors, landowners and nobility argued over who should be in charge of Jewish affairs.

### Small Triumphs

There were bright spots to come, though – Jewish people did enjoy golden periods of freedom under Emperor Rudolf II (r 1576–1612) and Mayor Mordechai Maisel (1528–1601) and Rabbi Loew (1525–1609; see p63). The city's Jewish population grew exponentially as refugees from Germany, Spain and Austria settled in Prague. Another triumph occurred in 1648, when Prague's Jewish citizens were credited with helping repel invading Swedes on Charles Bridge at the end of the Thirty Years' War.

Emancipation came from 1848, when the ghetto walls were torn down and the Jewish quarter renamed Josefov in honour of the emperor of the time. As wealthy Jews moved out the area slid into squalor. Between 1896 and 1910 this 'slum' was cleared and rebuilt in art-nouveau style.

### Elimination & Preservation

The community itself was all but eliminated by the Nazis, and today only some 6000 Jews remain in Prague. It's said the Nazis preserved the synagogues of today's Jewish Museum because, chillingly, they wanted to build a museum of an extinct race.

Philharmonic Orchestra, the venue's excellent reputation is also boosted by its sterling musicianship. (☏ 227 059 352; www.ceskafilharmonie.cz; náměstí Jana Palacha 1; tickets 250-600Kč; ☺box office 10am-6pm Mon-Fri; Ⓜ Staroměstská)

### Roxy
CLUB

**15** ⭐ Map p64, E2

In the shell of an art-deco cinema, its ramshackle nature is an integral part of the treasured Roxy's charm. There's a lounge-lizard bar and 'experimental arts space' NoD upstairs, while a vaguely themed 'ice bar' (with tacky fibreglass polar bear and foosball) leads off the large main floor. DJs spin house, trance, chill-out and more. Live bands also play and free Mondays attract droves of students. (☏ 224 826 296; www.roxy.cz; Dlouhá 33; cover Fri & Sat 150-250Kč, Mon free, other nights vary; ☺7pm-midnight Mon-Thu, to 6am Fri & Sat; Ⓜ Náměstí Republiky)

# Shopping

### Granát Turnov
JEWELLERY

**16** 🅰 Map p64, E3

The vast array of stores selling garnet jewellery in Prague is confusing, but this is the connoisseurs' favourite and it's easy to see why. As the largest national manufacturer, it has a huge range, from genuine gold and garnet pieces to more affordable gold-plated silver and *vltavín* (or moldavite, a dark-green semiprecious stone). Look

for the sign 'Bohemian Garnet Jewellery'. (www.granat.eu; Dlouhá 28; Ⓜ Náměstí Republiky or Staroměstská)

### Kebab
FASHION

**17** 🅰 Map p64, C3

The coolest streetwear boutique in Prague is notable for its stylish but humorous interior, courtesy of designer Maxim Velčoský (creator of the famous 'Pure' barcoded ceramic tumblers resembling disposable plastic cups). (www.kebabstore.cz; Dušní 13; Ⓜ Staroměstská)

### Qubus
ARTS & CRAFTS

**18** 🅰 Map p64, D3

Leading designers Maxim Velčoský and Jakob Berdych at Qubus offer Czech design pieces like ceramic *matryoshky*, cake-slice-shaped candleholders, wine glasses resembling throwaway plastic cups, liquid lights and Lomo cameras. (www.qubus.cz; Rámová 3; Ⓜ Staroměstská)

**Ⓠ Local Life**
### Bohemian Glass at Kotva

**Kotva** (www.od-kotva.cz; Náměstí Republiky 8; Ⓜ Náměstí Republiky) is a midrange Czech department store, unremarkable to tourists except for one notable section: several flights up, in housewares, is a wonderful selection of Bohemian crystal and glassware. This is the kind of place where locals pick up wedding gifts. Look for discounted champagne flutes, vases, decanters and martini glasses.

Explore

# Old Town Square & Staré Město

A charming labyrinth of narrow walkways, towering stone arches and petite plazas crowded with sidewalk cafes, Staré Město is the beating heart of Prague's historic quarter. Its centrepiece is the stunning Old Town Square, famous for its reputation as Frank Kafka's stomping grounds and for the fairy-tale Gothic spires that rise up from the Church of Our Lady Before Týn.

DOUG MCKINLAY/LONELY PLANET IMAGES ©

# The Sights in a Day

For the quietest experience and most magical views of **Charles Bridge** (p74), start your morning as early as possible. Start on the Malá Strana side and cross the bridge towards Old Town, then make a beeline for the **Astronomical Clock** (pictured left; p73) to catch the famous hourly chiming before the tourist crowds start to multiply. Afterwards, climb the **Old Town Hall Tower** (p73) for morning views over Old Town Sq and the historic centre.

Take a load off and have a leisurely lunch at **V Zátiší** (p79), sampling gourmet versions of Czech dishes from the tasting menu. Then wander the quaint cobblestoned backstreets around Betlémské náměstí, stopping for a coffee or to browse the boutiques along **Karolíny Světlé** (p81).

As night falls, head back to Old Town Sq to view the beautifully illuminated **Church of St Nicholas** (p73) and **Church of Our Lady Before Týn** (p73). Enjoy a glass of Moravian wine in a glamorous setting at **Municipal House Cafe** (p83) or catch some live jazz at **ArghaRTA Jazz Centrum** (p85) to finish off the day.

## 👁 Top Sights

Old Town Square & Astronomical Clock (p72)

Charles Bridge (p74)

## 💜 Best of Prague

**Bars & Pubs**
Grand Café Orient (p81)

Bar & Books (p81)

Municipal House Café (p83)

**Food**
Bellevue (p78)

Lehká Hlava (p79)

V Zátiší (p79)

Beas Vegetarian Dhaba (p80)

Klub Architektů (p80)

Ristorante Pasta Fresca (p80)

**Art**
Museum of Czech Cubism (p78)

*Hanging Out* sculpture (p78)

**Museums**
Charles Bridge Museum (p75)

## Getting There

**Ⓜ Metro** The most central stop is Staroměstská, on Line A. Others are Náměstí Republiky and Narodni Trida (both on Line B) and Můstek (Lines A and B).

## Top Sights
# Old Town Square & Astronomical Clock

Laid with cobblestones and surrounded by spectacular baroque churches, soaring spires, candy-coloured buildings and a rococo palace, Old Town Sq is an architectural smorgasbord and a photographer's delight. The 600th anniversary of the square's most famous attraction, the Astronomical Clock – a mechanical marvel that still chimes on the hour – was marked in 2010. But many of Old Town Sq's structures are even older: settlers started moving here, across the river from Prague Castle, in the 11th century.

👁 Map p76, C2

Old Town Sq

admission free

🕐 Old Town Hall Tower 11am-10pm Mon, 9am-10pm Tue-Sun

Ⓜ Staroměstská

Historic buildings from Old Town Hall Tower

# Don't Miss

### Astronomical Clock

Built in 1490 by a master clockmaker named Hanuš, the Astronomical Clock was a scientific feat in its day – and the relic, even after various renovations, remains a paradigm of antique technology and religious symbolism. A crowd gathers at the foot of the clock tower for a quaint visual display, the procession of the Twelve Apostles, during the hourly chiming (between 9am and 9pm).

### Church of Our Lady Before Týn

Straight out of a 15th-century fairy tale, the spiky, spooky Gothic spires of Týn Church are an unmistakable Old Town landmark. The church houses the tomb of Tycho Brahe (see p82); it's only open for services (check http://tynska.far nost.cz for times) but you can always peer through the glass doors.

### Old Town Hall Tower

Old Town Hall, dating from 1338, has more to offer than the astronomical clock. Climb the tall staircase of the **clock tower** (admission adult/concession 100/20Kč) for privileged views over Old Town Sq and the historic city centre.

### Church of St Nicholas

This pretty baroque monastery is relatively new: finished in 1735, it replaced a much older Gothic church built here in the late 13th century. It's gone through several reincarnations since, serving as a worship space for Catholics, Protestants, and even Prague's Russian Orthodox community before transitioning into a classical concert venue.

☑ **Top Tips**

▶ For the best views of the Astronomical Clock, come to the chiming at 9am or 10am. Arrive a few minutes before the hour.

▶ Look for lively food and craft stands in Old Town Sq around major holidays like Christmas and Easter.

▶ Climb the clock tower for spectacular views over Old Town Sq; again, earlier is better.

▶ The most romantic time to visit the square is after dark, when the medieval buildings are beautifully illuminated.

✗ **Take a Break**

Have lunch at Ristorante Pasta Fresca (p80), a modern classic just a block past Old Town Sq on busy Celetná street.

At night, have cocktails with a spectacular view of Old Town Sq atop Hotel U Prince (p78).

## Top Sights
# Charles Bridge

You know a historic landmark is something special when even the crush of tourist traffic hardly takes away from its magnificence. So it is with Charles Bridge, Prague's most legendary monument. Commissioned in 1357, the massive 520m-long stone bridge was the only link across the Vltava River between Prague Castle and the Old Town until 1741. It's particularly awe-inspiring at dawn, when the silhouettes of saintly statues along both sides seem to guide you toward the towering hilltop fortress.

⊙ Map p76, A2

Karluv Most; entry from Mostecká (in Malá Strana) and Karlova (in Staré Město)

admission free

Ⓜ Staroměstská

Charles Bridge with Old Town Bridge Tower and dome of Church of St Francis of Assisi

# Don't Miss

### Old Town Bridge Tower

Blackened with age, this Gothic tower on the Staré Město side of Charles Bridge was one of Prague's original town fortifications. It houses an **observation tower** (Staroměstské mostecká vez; adult/concession 70/50Kč; ⊙10am-10pm May-Sep, to 7pm Apr & Oct, to 6pm Mar, to 5pm Nov-Feb) with front-row views of the city's rooftops. You'll find a similar tower, also with an observation deck, on the Malá Strana side of the bridge.

### Saintly Statues

Most of the striking statues that line the bridge are just copies of the originals (many of which are now housed inside the National Museum, p95). But this stone pageant of saints is impressive nonetheless: look for the Madonna with a dog, a mournful rabbi, and St Francis of Assisi with a pair of angels.

### Stone Relief of John of Nepomuk

Midway down the bridge, you'll see people reaching out to place their hands on a burnished relief sculpture at the foot of the statue of St John of Nepomuk. It's said to be good luck to touch the portrayal of the saint's 1393 martyrdom – you'll see the same image on bridges all over Europe.

### Charles Bridge Museum

Examine the history of the Vltava's most famous crossing at **Charles Bridge Museum** (Muzeum Karlova mostu; www.muzeumkarlovamostu.cz; Křižovnické náměstí 3; adult/concession 150/70Kč; ⊙10am-8pm May-Sep, to 6pm Oct-Apr), located near the bridge's Old Town entrance. When you learn about the bridge's tumultuous 650-year history, you'll be surprised it's still standing.

## ☑ Top Tips

▶ Visit the bridge early in the day to beat the crowds.

▶ Keep your valuables close at hand; pickpockets lurk here, especially in summer.

▶ Plan to cross the bridge at least twice – once towards the castle and once away from it.

▶ Sunrise is the ideal time for photos. In winter, if it starts snowing, head for the bridge to capture some unforgettable images.

## ✕ Take a Break

Splurge on a gourmet meal paired with Czech wine at Bellevue (p78).

Relax over a coffee or beer at Duende (p83); in the evening, you might catch a live acoustic set.

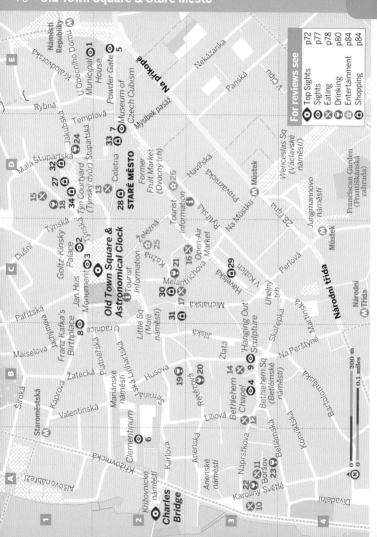

Náměstí Republiky ⓜ

U Obecního Domu ⓜ

Municipal House ◉1

Powder Gate ◉5

Na příkopě

Museum of Czech Cubism ◉7

Nekázanka

Panská

V Cípu

Rybná

Jakubská

Templová

Malá Štupartská

Celetná ◉33

Haštalská

STARÉ MĚSTO

Former Fruit Market (Ovocný trh)

Myslbek pasáž

Havířská

Ⓜ Můstek

27 32

15 ⊗

18 ⊗ 34

Týnská

Tyn Courtyard (Týnský dvůr)

Štupartská

◉13

◉28

Železná

◉25

Kožná

Ovocný trh

Ⓜ Můstek

Wenceslas Sq (Václavské náměstí)

Jungmannovo náměstí

Franciscan Garden (Františkánská zahrada)

Goltz-Kinsky Palace ◉2

Týnská

Tourist Information ⓘ

Tourist Information

21 ⊗

16 ⊗ Open-Air Market

Rytířská

Na Můstku

Provaznická

Dušní

Jan Hus Monument ◉3

**Old Town Square & Astronomical Clock**

Melantrichova

30

17 ⊗

31

Havelská

V kotcích ⊗29

Uhelný trh

Perlova

Parížská

Franz Kafka's Birthplace ◉8

Radnice

Little Sq (Malé náměstí) ⓘ

Jilská

Michalská

Skořepka

Martinská

Národní třída

Maiselova

Jáchymova

Platnéřská

U radnice

Husova

Řetězová

Zlatá

'Hanging Out' Sculpture ◉9

Na Perštýně

Ⓜ Národní Třída

Žatecká

Mariánské náměstí

Linhartská

Seminářská

19 ⊗

◉20

Bethlehem 14 ⊗

Chapel ◉4

Bethlehem Sq (Betlémské náměstí)

Konviktská

Bartolomějská

Široká

Kaprova

Valentinská

Staroměstská Ⓜ

Seminářská

Liliová

Betlémská

200 m

0.1 miles

Klementinum ◉6

Karlova

Anenská

Náprstkova

Bořšov ◉23

22 ⊗

11 ⊗

◉10

Karoliny Světlé

Křížovnická

Staroměstská Ⓜ

Alšovo nábřeží

Křížovnické náměstí

**Charles Bridge**

Anenské náměstí

Divadelní

# Sights

## Municipal House HISTORIC SITE

1  Map p76, E1

An art-nouveau expression of national aspirations, the ornate Municipal House is laden with symbolism; the *Homage to Prague* mosaic above the entrance is set between sculptures representing the oppression and rebirth of the Czech people. Visit the cafe (p83), catch a concert in Smetana Hall or book a tour at the information office (to the left of the lobby stairs). (Obecní dům; ☎ 222 002 101; www.obecni-dum.cz; náměstí Republiky 5; tours incl a drink in the American Cafe adult/concession 280/230Kč; ☺building 7.30am-11pm, information centre 10am-7pm, daily tour times vary; MNáměstí Republiky)

## Goltz-Kinsky Palace HISTORIC SITE

2  Map p76, C1

The wealthy Count Goltz commissioned this pink-and-white rococo palace in 1755; the Kinsky family later took up residence through 1945. The palace has claims to fame – a young Franz Kafka attended school in the building, and later, in 1948, prominent politician Klement Gottwald took to the balcony to announce the beginning of the communist era in Prague. (Palac Goltz-Kinskych; Staroměstské namestí; MStaroměstská)

## Jan Hus Monument MONUMENT

3  Map p76, C1

This moving stone monument pays tribute to the one-time dean of Charles University. Hus condemned the church for selling indulgences before being burned at the stake for heresy in 1415, an event that prompted the Protestant rebellion called the 'Hussite Wars'. The memorial was unveiled in 1915, exactly 500 years after Hus' death. (Staroměstské namestí; MStaroměstská)

## Bethlehem Chapel CHURCH

4  Map p76, B3

Although a reconstruction, this barn-like church uses the pulpit and some original walls from the 3000-seater where the great Czech reformer Jan Hus preached from 1402 to 1412. (Betlémská kaple; Betlémské náměstí 3; adult/child 50/30Kč; ☺10am-6.30pm Tue-Sun Apr-Oct, to 5.30pm Tue-Sun Nov-Mar; MNárodní Třída)

## Powder Gate HISTORIC SITE

5  Map p76, E2

Built in the 15th century over one of the Old Town's original 13 gates, the 65m Powder Gate derives its name from its role as a gunpowder store in the 18th century. Given a neo-Gothic makeover 100 years later, it towers dramatically over the western end of busy Na příkopě. (Prašná brána; Na příkopě; adult/concession 70/50Kč; ☺10am-6pm Apr-Oct; MNáměstí Republiky)

## Clementinum

HISTORIC SITE

6  Map p76, A2

A monastery-turned–Jesuit university that expanded significantly (in both size and power) during the later 17th century, this sprawling historic complex boasts the National Library and an interesting astronomical tower. These two spaces are only available for viewing through a guided tour; another way to get into the Clementinum is to get tickets for classical concerts held in the lovely Mirror Chapel. (Klementinum; Křižovnická 190, Karlova 1; tours adult/concession 220/140Kč; ⏱10am-5pm, concerts at 5pm or 6pm; Ⓜ Staroměstská)

## Museum of Czech Cubism

MUSEUM

7  Map p76, D2

A proud reminder that the Czechs were the only people to apply cubist principles to architecture and furniture, Josef Gočár's 1912 House of the Black Madonna – itself strikingly angular – has three floors of oddly shaped ceramics, glassware, paintings, chairs and sofas you wouldn't want to get into an argument with. (Muzeum Českého kubismu; www.ngprague.cz; House of the Black Madonna, Ovocný trh 19; adult/child 100/50Kč; ⏱10am-6pm Tue-Sun; Ⓜ Náměstí Republiky)

## Franz Kafka's Birthplace

HISTORIC SITE

8  Map p76, B1

An oft-photographed bust of the great writer marks the building where he was born on 3 July 1883, at what was then U Radnice 5. Now, this spot in the shadow of the Old Town Sq's Church of St Nicholas is named after him. (Náměstí Franze Kafky 3; Ⓜ Staroměstská)

## Hanging Out Sculpture

PUBLIC ART

9  Map p76, B3

Here's more inspired madness from artist David Černý (p45 and p116). Look up at this corner; you'll see a bearded, bespectacled chap not unlike Sigmund Freud casually dangling by one hand from a pole way above the street. In Czech the 1997 *Hanging Out* is called *Viselec*. (Viselec; cnr Husova & Skořepka; Ⓜ Národní Třída)

# Eating

## Bellevue

FRENCH €€€

10 🍴 Map p76, A3

Book a table on the terrace and come to enjoy the fabulous views of the

---

☑️ Top Tip

**Top Views Of Old Town Square**

The food might not be brilliant atop **U Prince** (Map p76, C4; 🕿 224 213 807; www.hoteluprince.com; Staroměstské náměstí 29), but the bird's-eye view of Old Town Sq is unforgettable. Find its rooftop terrace by taking the lift at the back of the entrance hall to the top and climbing the stairs from there.

CHRISTER FREDRIKSSON/LONELY PLANET IMAGES ©

The roofs and church towers of Old Town

river and castle while tucking into gourmet cuisine. Bellevue offers a Eurasian choice of dishes from roasted veal loin in black-truffle crust to New Zealand lamb chops marinated in lemon thyme. For a truly leisurely meal, try a seasonal tasting menu with wine pairing. (📞224 221 443; www.zatisi group.cz; Smetanovo nábr 18; ☾lunch & dinner; 🚋17, 18 to Karlovy lázně; 🗷)

## Lehká Hlava
VEGETARIAN €€

11 🍴 Map p76, A3

Despite some hippy talk of 'delighting your soul' and 'supporting your whole body', 'Clear Head' proves quite chic. Set in a historic house down a side street, this vegetarian favourite has an international menu, colourful walls, tables inlaid with clear marbles (faintly glowing ultraviolet) and artistic videos projected on the walls. The set lunch (108 Kč) on weekdays is a steal. (www.lehkahlava.cz; Boršov 2/280; ☾lunch & dinner; 🚋17, 18 to Karlovy lázně; ⊖🗷🚺)

## V Zátiší
CZECH, INTERNATIONAL €€€

12 🍴 Map p76, B3

Foodies praise the rotating Czech and international menu at this refined eatery. The cuisine changes according to visiting talent: at the time of writing, an esteemed Indian chef added lamb lime curry and tandoori tiger prawns to the list of well-prepared Bohemian dishes. (📞222 221 155; www.vzatisi.cz; Liliová 1; ☾lunch & dinner; Ⓜ Můstek)

### Understand
## Time's Arrow

Its upper disc is the only original element of Prague's Astronomical Clock (p73). The figures of the Turk, Death, Greed and Vanity beside it were added in the 1800s. The figures of the 12 apostles, which appear hourly, and the lower calendar disc, with 12 monthly scenes of rural life by artist Josef Mánes, are both 19th-century additions.

The three hands on the upper face measure solar, lunar and stellar movements. The sun-hand points to the hour on the Roman-numeral ring; the top XII is noon and the bottom XII is midnight. The mini-sun on the same pointer traces a circle through the blue zone of day, the brown zone of dusk (Crepusculum in Latin) in the west (Occasus), the black vector of night, and dawn (Aurora) in the east (Ortus). From this, the hours of sunrise and sunset can be read.

Likewise, the moon-hand traces a path through day and night. The small moving ring in the middle of the face marks the zodiac, and the position of the mini-sun and mini-moon over it indicates which house of the zodiac each is in.

## Ristorante Pasta Fresca
ITALIAN €€

13 🍴 Map p76, D2

One of several stylish (and perhaps overly popular) eateries in the Ambiente chain, Pasta Fresca is a solid choice for an Italian lunch of gourmet pizza or perfectly al dente spaghetti. Its greatest selling point? The location just around the corner from Old Town Sq. (www.ambi.cz; Celetná 11; ☺lunch & dinner; Ⓜ Náměstí Republiky; 🛜🍴)

## Klub Architektů
INTERNATIONAL €€

14 🍴 Map p76, B3

Trust an architects' society to combine a candlelit 12th-century cellar with exposed industrial ducting and modern metalwork. The extensive menu caters for vegetarians and vegans as well as carnivores; as in any place with a big menu, the daily specials are always a good idea. (www.klubarchitektu.com; Betlémské náměstí 5; ☺lunch & dinner; Ⓜ Národní Třída; ➖🍴)

## Beas Vegetarian Dhaba
VEGETARIAN €

15 🍴 Map p76, D1

Tucked away in a quiet courtyard off Týnská, this friendly, informal Indian restaurant offers self-service vegetarian curries served with rice, salad, and chutneys. It's a great budget-friendly lunch option if you're looking to splash out somewhere flashier for dinner. (www.beas-dhaba.cz; Týnská 19; ☺lunch & dinner Mon-Sat, lunch Sun; Ⓜ Náměstí Republiky; 🍴)

## U Zavoje
FRENCH €€€

**16**  Map p76, C3

Set in a quiet lane between Havelská and Kožná streets, U Zavoje is a versatile space: it's a wine bar, restaurant, coffeehouse and delicatessen all at once. The menu features French flavours with an emphasis on seasonal and local produce. Try the grilled swordfish with pistachio risotto; ask the sommelier for a recommendation from the impressive French- and Czech-centric wine cellar. (☑226 006 120; www.uzavoje.cz; Havelská 25; ☺noon-midnight; Ⓜ Můstek)

## Country Life
VEGETARIAN €

**17** Map p76, C2

At this veteran health-food hub, the pay-by-weight buffet of salads, tofu burgers and hot dishes brings in a steady crowd of locals and expats. It's a convenient spot to pick up a few dishes for an alfresco picnic lunch by the river. (www.countrylife.cz; Melantrichova 15; ☺lunch & dinner Sat-Thu, lunch only Fri; Ⓜ Můstek; ☝)

# Drinking

## Grand Café Orient
CAFE

Reopened in 2005 after an 80-year closure, this stunning cubist gem near the Museum of Czech Cubism (see 7 ◉ Map p76, D2) features Josef Gočár's original designs, with striking green lampshades, striped upholstery and angular wooden bar and coathooks. The result is swish and unique, and the sunny balcony and patio are popular with both locals and tourists. (www.grandcafeorient.cz; House of the Black Madonna, Ovocný trh 19; Ⓜ Náměstí Republiky; ☝)

## Bar & Books
BAR

**18** Map p76, D1

Dust off your James Bond fantasies at this luscious, library-themed Old

### ◯ Local Life
### Karolíny Světlé

This narrow, snaking street is home to several independent design shops, hipster bars and arty cafes that run all the way between Náprstkova and Národní třída. Along with Duende (p83), look out for the following establishments as you're getting pleasantly lost.

**Kabul** (Map p76, A3; www.kabulrestaurant.cz; Karolíny Světlé 14; ☝) Delightful Afghan restaurant with a pretty interior courtyard.

**Standard Café** (Map p76, A3; www.standardcafe.cz; Karolíny Světlé 23; ☝☝) A hip and colourful cafe with appealing sidewalk tables and a varied list of coffee, beer and wine.

**Nábytek ProByt** (Map p76, A3; Krocínova 5, cnr Karolíny Světlé; ☺closed Sun) Interesting homewares store; the cool retro advertising signs will catch your eye.

> Understand
>
> ## The Trials of Tycho Brahe
>
> It's fair to describe Tycho Brahe, who's buried in the Church of Our Lady Before Týn (p73), as something of a character. This Danish father of modern astronomy catalogued thousands of stars, made stunningly accurate observations in an era before telescopes, and helped his assistant Johannes Kepler derive the laws of planetary motion. He came to Prague in 1599 as Emperor Rudolf II's official mathematician.
>
> But Brahe also dabbled in astrology and alchemy. He lost part of his nose in a duel and wore a metal replacement. His pet moose drank too much beer, fell down the stairs and died. In Prague, Brahe himself died in 1601 of a bladder infection, reputedly because he was too polite to go to the toilet during a long banquet. Only recently have historians decided he was probably poisoned instead.

Town cocktail bar bedecked with leather seating and stunning crimson decor. Prices are a little steep – think London or New York, rather than Prague – but it's worth popping in for at least one well-mixed cocktail. (www.barandbooks.cz/tynska; Týnská 19; Náměstí Republiky; 🛜)

## U Zlatého Tygra
PUB

**19**  Map p76, B2

Václav Havel brought fellow president Bill Clinton here in 1994 to show him a real Czech pub. Today, it's all in the timing, or perhaps sheer luck, whether you find the 'Golden Tiger' full of tourists or having an authentic moment (weekday evenings are your best bet). This was novelist Bohumil Hrabal's favourite drinking hole – note a bust of him on the wall. (www.uzlatehotygra.cz; Husova 17; Ⓜ️Staroměstská)

## Literární Kavárna Řetězová
CAFE

**20** 🛜 Map p76, B3

This is where you would have headed post-1989 to become the next great expat novelist. Two decades on, leave your laptop at home, take in the vintage black-and-white pics of famous Czech writers, and treat yourself to a coffee or a *kvasnicové* (yeast beer) from the Bernard brewery. (Řetězová 10; 🕐noon-11pm Mon-Fri, 5-11pm Sat & Sun; Ⓜ️Staroměstská)

## Čili Bar
BAR

**21** 🛜 Map p76, C2

This raffish bar is more Žižkov than Staré Město, with cool cocktails and a grungy tinge in welcome contrast to the crystal shops and Russian dolls around the corner. Relax in comfy old armchairs from your first student flat, and surprise yourself with Čili's signature tipple – a shot of rum laced with diced chillies. The owner has worked and travelled around the world, so you should have loads in common after a few drinks. (www.cilibar.cz; Kožná 8; M Můstek)

## Duende
BAR

22 ⦿ Map p76, A3

Bedecked with intriguing photos and all matter of quirky ephemera, this bohemian drinking den attracts an arty, local crowd of all ages. They come for a chat, a glass of wine or to take in acoustic music performances, ranging from guitar to violin. (www.barduende.cz; Karolíny Světlé 30; M Národní Třída)

## Municipal House Café
CAFE

Everyone should visit this legendary Viennese-style coffeehouse in Municipal House (see 1 ⦿ Map p76, E1) at least once. With its opulent Secessionist fittings and its formally dressed staff, it certainly looks a picture, and it has historical import. As with many venues this well known, however, the coffee can be lousy and the service lax. (www.obecni-dum.cz; Náměstí Republiky 5; M Náměstí Republiky; 🛜 📶 🚻)

## Pražský Most U Valšů
PUB

23 ⦿ Map p76, A3

One of Prague's newest brewpubs is located on a quiet street on the southern edge of the Old Town. Four

Cobblestone passageway, Old Town

Understand
## Literary Prague

The late Alan Levy, former editor of the *Prague Post,* dubbed Prague 'the Left Bank of the 1990s' early in that decade. This stirring notion was forged by the prominent role of writers in the Czechoslovak anticommunist resistance, from Charta 77 onwards, and by seeing playwright Václav Havel in the presidential hot seat. Aiding and abetting the Paris myth were the many undergraduates thumbing Milan Kundera (*The Unbearable Lightness of Being*) and Ivan Klíma (*Love and Garbage*) in the early 1990s. So where did it all begin?

### Early Influences
The oldest known texts in the former Czechoslovakia, dating from the 8th century, are translations of religious documents from Latin into Slavic. At the beginning of the 15th century, trends shifted as Jan Hus published his theological and reformatory writings. Hus established grammatical rules that changed modern Czech language, including his reintroduction of diacritics, or symbols that represent sounds, back into common usage.

### The Nation's New Literature
The baroque era's Protestant and Catholic writings gave way to an age of enlightenment – a time when public citizens started reading. Texts written in Czech, as opposed to German, gained value, and writing was slowly accepted as a form of artistic expression; this social mentality stirred national pride in a new, lyrical form of Czech literature.

### The Golden Age
Further adding to the Czech nationalist tradition were social anarchist Jaroslav Hašek, known for his novel *The Good Soldier Švejk,* and Jan Neruda, 19th-century author of short stories and satires; Chilean poet Pablo Neruda so admired the writer that he took his name as a pseudonym. Considered one of the finest writers of his time, Bohumil Hrabal wrote several famous novels; his *Closely Observed Trains* was adapted into a script that won an Oscar in 1967. The era's heaviest hitter was Franz Kafka, the Jewish antibureaucrat who attended school in Old Town Sq and later wrote *Metamorphosis*. As most of his work was published against his wishes – that is to say, posthumously – his genius wasn't recognised in his lifetime.

different beers and well-priced Czech food, including vegetarian dishes, are on offer. Decor is a modern spin on medieval, and the standout brew on offer is the tasty *tmavé pivo* (dark beer). An upstairs garden is a draw in summertime. (www.prazskymost.cz; Betlémská 5; ⏰11am-11pm; Ⓜ Národní Třída)

### Chapeau Rouge CLUB
26  Map p76, D1

This raucous, smoke-filled corner lounge and club, with fading blood-red walls and a crowd of expats lining up at the bar, has three levels hosting everything from hardcore and indie rock to samba and Balkan house. Its central location is an asset when you've had one too many; lots of Old Town hotels are a short walk away. (www.chapeaurouge.cz; Jakubská 2; Ⓜ Náměstí Republiky)

## Entertainment

### AghaRTA Jazz Centrum CLUB
25 ⭐ Map p76, C2

AghaRTA has been staging top-notch modern Czech jazz, blues, funk and fusion since 1991, and moved into this venue in 2004. A typical jazz cellar with red-brick vaults and a cosy bar and cafe, it hosts local and international artists – the place draws big names every autumn during its annual Jazz Festival. (📞222 211 275; www.agharta.cz; Železná 16; ⏰7pm-1am, music 9pm-midnight; Ⓜ Můstek)

### Estates Theatre CONCERT HALL
26  Map p76, D2

This is the small but beautifully decorated theatre where Mozart premiered and personally conducted *Don Giovanni* on 29 October 1787. Although much of today's program consists of second-rate Mozart homages – where you want to leave after 10 minutes – it is possible to see some good performances, including some ballets. (Stavovské divadlo; 📞224 902 322; www.estatestheatre.cz; Ovocny trh; Ⓜ Můstek)

### Smetana Hall CONCERT HALL
Acoustics? Who cares about slightly imperfect acoustics when a concert hall looks this good? Decorated with stunning ceiling murals, the 1200-seat Smetana Hall in Municipal House (see 1  Map p76, E1) creates sufficient atmosphere on its own. House musicians the Prague Symphony Orchestra kick off the Prague Spring music festival here annually. Day-to-day performers are often less experienced. (📞220 002 101; www.obecni-dum.cz; Municipal House, Náměstí Republiky 5; Ⓜ Náměstí Republiky)

## Shopping
### Botanicus COSMETICS
27 🔒 Map p76, D1

Prepare for olfactory overload in this popular old apothecary, selling natural health and beauty products in rustic-chic packaging. The scented soaps, herbal bath oils and shampoos,

RICHARD NEBESKY/LONELY PLANET IMAGES ©

Crystal shop display

fruit cordials and handmade paper products are made from herbs and plants grown on an organic farm east of Prague. (www.botanicus.cz; Týn 3; Ⓜ Náměstí Republiky)

## Modernista
ARTS & CRAFTS

**28** 🔒 Map p76, D2

This classy showcase of Czech cubist and art-deco design features cool yet affordable ceramics, jewellery, posters and books. Early-20th-century reproductions include wooden toys (Ladislav Sutnar), cubist boxes (Pavel Janák), expressionist ashtrays (Vlastislav Hofman), and Jindrich Halabala's iconic 1931 reclining armchair. Contemporary items like sperm-shaped teaspoons and Škoda toy cars add humour. (www.modernista.cz; Celetná 12; Ⓜ Náměstí Republiky)

## Havelská Market
ARTS & CRAFTS

**29** 🔒 Map p76, C3

Skip the cheesy souvenir shops surrounding this daily open-air market and head straight for the good stuff. Browsing through the market stalls, you'll find fresh honey, traditional sweets and liqueurs, colourfully painted wooden kitchenware, and a variety of Czech-style treats and home accessories. (Havelská; Ⓜ Můstek)

## Manufaktura
ARTS & CRAFTS

**30** 🔒 Map p76, C2

The largest of several Manufaktura stores across town, this shop is an inviting emporium of Czech traditional crafts, featuring wooden toys, scented soaps, beeswax candles, ceramics, 'blue' printed fabrics, Bohemian lacework and more. (www.manufaktura.cz; Melantrichova 17; **M** Můstek)

## Art Deco Galerie
ANTIQUES

**31** 🔒 Map p76, C2

This shop has 1920s and '30s art-deco goodies including clothes, handbags, jewellery, glassware and ceramics. A few minutes' leisurely browsing is bound to reveal something you simply *can't* live without. (www.artdecogalerie -mili.com; Michalská 21; **M** Můstek)

## Big Ben
BOOKS

**32** 🔒 Map p76, D1

A small but very well stocked English-language bookshop, Big Ben also sells English-language newspapers and magazines at the counter. (www.bigben bookshop.com; Malá Štupartská 5; **M** Náměstí Republiky)

## Pohádka
TOYS

**33** 🔒 Map p76, D2

This store is sometimes beset by souvenir-hunting tour groups and it stocks plenty of *matryoshky* (Russian stacking dolls) – objects that actually have nothing to do with Prague. Surprisingly, then, it's also a pretty good place to shop for genuine Czech toys, from marionettes and costumed dolls to finger puppets, rocking horses and toy cars. (www.czechtoys.cz; Celetná 32; **M** Náměstí Republiky)

## Material
GLASSWARE

**34** 🔒 Map p76, D1

Material puts a modern twist on the Czech crystal industry, with its oversized contemporary vases, bowls and Dale Chihuly–like ornaments, candleholders, chandeliers and glasses. The firm boasts its 'drunken sailor' glass is spillproof. Yet, despite well-spaced displays, it's a store where you immediately fear breaking something – and when you check the prices you realise you should! (www.i-material.com; Týn 1; **M** Náměstí Republiky)

Explore

# Wenceslas Square & Around

Busy Wenceslas Sq, dating from 1348 and once a bustling horse market, was the site of several seminal events in Czech history. Today, though it's crowded with souvenir shops, nightclubs, coffee chains, sausage stands and plenty of tourists, it's possible to glimpse the square's previous grandeur simply by looking up at the glorious art-nouveau architecture.

RICHARD NEBESKY/LONELY PLANET IMAGES ©

# The Sights in a Day

☀ Start the day with breakfast at **Bibita Nuova** (p95), then walk over to **Wenceslas Square** (p90). Climb the steps of the **National Museum** (p95, currently closed for renovations) to take in views of the square, including the **Radio Free Europe Building** (p91). Check out the **Wenceslas Statue** (p91) and the **Jan Palach Memorial** (p91). Marvel at the art-nouveau architecture of **Kavárna Evropa** (p91) and the buildings around it, but don't stop for coffee there – cross the square and loop around to **Kavárna Lucerna** (p96) to enjoy an espresso in the slightly shabby old-world cafe.

☀ Wander around the square's shops – don't miss **Bat'a** (p98) – then head over to **U Ferdinanda** (p95) for a classic Czech lunch. Walk down the street to the **Mucha Museum** (p93) to admire the painter's dreamlike beauties emblazoned on early-20th-century Paris posters.

☾ After dinner at **Kogo** (p95), head over to the gorgeous **State Opera House** (p98) to see a performance of ballet or opera. Alternatively, catch a Czech film subtitled in English at **Kino Světozor** (p97), then drop by **U Pinkasů** (p96) for a beer at one of the city's most famous pubs.

For a local's walk in Wenceslas Sq area, see p98.

👁 **Top Sights**

 **Best of Prague**

## Getting There

**M Metro** Lines A and B converge at Můstek. Lines A and C converge at Muzeum.

## Top Sights
# Wenceslas Square

This massive central square was founded by Charles IV in 1348. For hundreds of years it was called the 'Horse Market' and featured a small lake, horse-drawn trams and the first Czech theatre. In medieval times it was also the site of several public executions. On 28 October 1918 the independent republic of Czechoslovakia was announced here; in 1945 the end of WWII was declared and celebrated. Later, during the Velvet Revolution, the square hosted huge, historic demonstrations.

⊙ Map p92, C3

Václavské náměstí

Ⓜ Můstek or Muzeum

National Museum (p95) and Wenceslas Statue

# Don't Miss

### Jan Palach Memorial
On 16 January 1969 university student Jan Palach set fire to himself in protest against the Soviet invasion of Czechoslovakia the preceding August. He died three days later. The exact spot the martyr fell is marked by a wooden cross in the pavement that seems to have suffered a small earthquake beneath it. Now 19 January is commemorated annually.

### Radio Free Europe Building
During the Cold War, US-financed Radio Free Europe was the most famous voice broadcasting from the capitalist West to the communist East. After 1989 it moved from Munich to Prague, into the former communist parliament. In 2009 the organisation occupied a new building in the Prague suburb of Hagibor. The 1970s glass-fronted building is now part of the neighbouring National Museum (p95).

### Wenceslas Statue
The focal point of Wenceslas Sq is this equestrian statue of St Wenceslas at its southern end. Sculptor Josef Myslbek has surrounded the 10th-century duke of Bohemia and the 'Good King Wenceslas' with four other patron saints of Bohemia – Prokop, Adalbert, Agnes and Ludmila.

### Kavárna Evropa
This ornate art-nouveau hotel and cafe is something of a tourist trap these days, but don't miss a chance to marvel at its fading grandeur from the pavement (and take another look at the bigger picture from across the square, too). Also note the colourful architecture surrounding this structure – it's easy to miss if you don't look up.

## ☑ Top Tips

▶ During holidays and festivals, try the square's food and drink stands for local specialities like spiced wine and grilled sausage.

▶ Keep an eye on your belongings – the square is notorious for pickpockets.

▶ Most of the square's restaurants are tourist traps; better-value options are nearby.

▶ The square gets seedier as the night goes on; beware of aggressive club promoters and drunken male tourist groups.

## ✕ Take a Break

At any time of day, step into Kavárna Lucerna (p96) for a coffee, a beer or a glass of wine in a darkened old-world atmosphere – the Lucerna Passage entrance is right on the square.

Just a block off Wenceslas Sq, Noodles (p95) offers excellent lunch specials and a relaxing garden – it's a huge leap above the nearby tourist offerings.

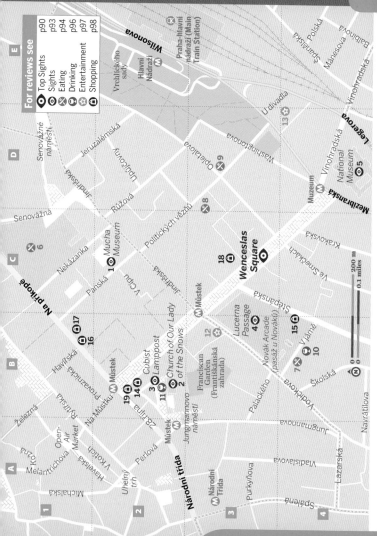

# Sights

## Mucha Museum                    MUSEUM

1 ◉ Map p92, C2

Sensuous Slavic maidens and fin-de-siècle Parisian adverts line the walls of this petite gallery housed in the lovely Kaunický Palace; whether or not you're an art-nouveau fan, it's worthwhile to walk through and see what the Mucha fuss is all about. Fans of the artist can call ahead to arrange a guided visit, or catch a screening of a short film about the artist's life. (☏221 451 333; www.mucha.cz; Panská 7; adult/student 180/120Kč; ⊙10am-6pm; Ⓜ Můstek)

## Church of Our Lady of the Snows                CHURCH

2 ◉ Map p92, B2

Fenced in by other buildings, this 14th-century church is easily overlooked, but shouldn't be. Charles IV planned it as Prague's largest church, but only its chancel was ever finished. So it seems taller than it is long, with an Orthodox Christian-style over-door mosaic and an ornate black-and-gold altarpiece. Enter via the Austrian Cultural Institute (Österreiches Kulturforum). (Kostel Panny Marie Sněžné; www.pms.ofm.cz; Jungmannovo náměstí; ⊙9am-6pm; Ⓜ Můstek)

## Cubist Lamppost               PUBLIC ART

3 ◉ Map p92, B2

Angular but slightly chunky, made from striated concrete – the world's only cubist lamppost would be worth going out of the way to see. So it's a happy bonus this novelty is just around the corner from Wenceslas Sq. (Jungmannovo náměstí; Ⓜ Můstek)

## Lucerna Passage            HISTORIC SITE

4 ◉ Map p92, B3

This 1920s art-nouveau shopping arcade, running below the Lucerna Palace between Štěpánská and Vodičkova streets, was designed by ex-president Havel's grandfather, but is now better known for a cafe (p96), a club (p97) and the David Černý sculpture *Horse* (1999). Hanging from the atrium, this wry

### Understand

### Overhaul of the National Museum

The hulking National Museum (p95) was opened in 1891 as a symbol of Czech-ness but 130 years later, it's a little unsteady on its foundations and needs a facelift. The museum is undergoing five years of renovation from 2011, during which time key exhibits will be relocated next door at the National Museum New Building. Following the renovation, which includes interactive exhibitions and new restaurants, the museum's collections will gradually move back into their original home and occupy both buildings.

## Understand

## Oppression & Revolution

### Communism & Resistance

February 1948 marked the start of a half century's worth of political turmoil in Prague. It was on this date that the Czech Communist Party, not content with a controlling position in the postwar coalition after the 1946 elections, staged a coup d'état that was backed by the Soviet Union. The next decade and a half saw widespread political persecution.

In the late 1960s national Communist Party leader Alexander Dubček loosened the reins slightly under the banner of 'socialism with a human face'. There was a cultural resurgence in literature, theatre and film, led by the likes of Milan Kundera, Bohumil Hrabal, Václav Havel and Miloš Forman. The Soviet regime crushed this 'Prague Spring' on 20 August 1968, using Warsaw Pact tanks, and Dubček was replaced by the orthodox Gustáv Husák.

### Velvet Revolution

In January 1977 a document called Charta 77 was signed by 243 intellectuals and artists, including Václav Havel. On 17 November 1989 a violent police attack on a peaceful Prague rally prompted the mass public support the resistance needed, by sparking continuous public demonstrations on Wenceslas Sq, and a 750,000-strong rally on Letná plain (25 and 26 November).

A group led by Havel procured the government's resignation on 3 December, and 26 days later he was the new leader. The 'Velvet Revolution' – named for its peaceful nature and the inspirational role of psychedelic '60s band the Velvet Underground – had succeeded.

### Velvet Divorce

The smoothness of both the revolution and the initial transition to a free market made Czechs the poster children for the postcommunist world in the early 1990s. But the fairy-tale ending everyone was hoping for never completely arrived.

The Slovak and Czech nations did divorce peacefully on 1 January 1993, and Prague became capital of the new Czech Republic with Václav Havel as president.

companion to the Wenceslas Sq statue has its Wenceslas (or Václav) astride the belly of a dead, upside-down steed. (Lucerna pasáž; Štěpánská 61/Vodičkova 36; M Můstek, ☐ 3, 9, 14, 24 to Václavské náměstí)

## National Museum
MUSEUM

 5 Map p92, D4

At the time of writing, the stately National Museum – presiding tall and proud over Wenceslas Sq – had closed for extensive renovations that were set to be completed in 2015. In the meantime, see natural-history exhibits across the street at the **National Museum New Building** (☎ 224 497 111; www.nm.cz; Vinohradská 1; adult/concession 100/70 Kč; ⏰ 10am-6pm, to 8pm 1st Wed of month, closed 1st Tue of month; M Muzeum). And even though the main museum is closed, you can still take in the expansive views of the square from the building's front steps. (Národní muzeum; Václavské náměstí)

# Eating

## Kogo
ITALIAN €€

6 Map p92, C1

Although its shopping-mall location doesn't seem promising at first, Kogo is a local favourite thanks to its relaxed Italian-style atmosphere and top-notch pizza, pasta, steak, seafood and winelist. (In summertime, score a courtyard table and you'll really forget you're in a mall.) (www.kogo.cz; Slovanský dům, Na příkopě 22; mains 285-510 Kč; M Náměstí Republiky; ☎ ✏ ♿)

## Bibita Nuova
ITALIAN €

7 Map p92, B4

This sleek new Italian coffee bar-eatery, with a contemporary dining room and a small side patio, features appetising (and well-priced) risotto, grilled steaks, fresh salads and paper-thin pizzas. It's pleasantly quiet and stylish, especially considering its location around the corner from Wenceslas Sq. (www.bibitanuova .cz; V jámě 8; mains 95-285 Kč; M Muzeum; ☎)

## Noodles
INTERNATIONAL €

8 Map p92, D3

In the stylish Hotel Yasmin, Noodles has a retro design (including large, furry blood-orange triffidlike sculptures) and a menu that uses a very broad definition of noodles, listing Italian pasta alongside Indonesian *bami goreng*, Japanese *yaki udon* and even Mongolian *tsuivan* noodles. (www.noodles.cz; Politických vězňů 12; mains 160-270 Kč; M Muzeum; ☎ ✏)

## U Ferdinanda
CZECH €

9 Map p92, D3

Welcome to a modern spin on a classic Czech pub, with beer courtesy of the Ferdinand brewery in nearby Benešov. Quirky gardening implements and lots of corrugated iron decorate the raucous interior, and a younger local clientele crowds in for well-priced Czech food. Don't leave without trying the 'Sedm Kulí' beer – named after the seven bullets that killed Franz Ferdinand (the Archduke, not the band). (cnr Opletalova & Politických vězňů; mains 135-200; M Muzeum)

# Drinking

### Jáma
BAR

10 🚇 Map p92, B4

This buzzing American expat bar and restaurant (the name is Czech for 'the Hollow') also attracts young Czechs with its leafy mini beer garden and mix of Pilsner Urquell, Gambrinus and Velkopopvický Kozel. With tasty burgers, steaks, ribs and chicken wings for the hungry. (www.jamapub.cz; V jámě 7; Ⓜ Muzeum, night tram 55, 56, 58; 🛜)

### Kavárna Lucerna
CAFE

A pre-cinema crowd joins card players, chain-smokers and barflies in this wonderfully atmospheric cafe, located in the slightly shabby art-nouveau Lucerna Passage (see 4 ◉ Map p92, B3), where light filtered through the yellow cupola and dirty-coloured fake marble create an aura of bittersweet nostalgia. Chocolate cake or *mednovík* are pretty

well the only nonliquid choices as you peer through the arched windows at David Černý's fibreglass *Horse*. (www .restaurace-monarchie.cz/kavarna-lucerna; Lucerna pasáž, Štěpánská 61/Vodičkova 36; Ⓜ Můstek, 🚊 3, 9, 14, 24 to Václavské náměstí)

### U Pinkasů
PUB

11 🚇 Map p92, B2

Allegedly Prague's oldest Pilsner pub (it was established in 1843), this was another haunt of writer Bohumil Hrabal. Also to its credit is that it's a *tankovna* pub selling particularly tasty unpasteurised pilsner, which is called *'hladinky'* by regulars. (www .upinkasu.cz; Jungmannovo náměstí 16; Ⓜ Můstek)

### Lucerna Music Bar
CLUB

An old theatre turned into a nightclub, Lucerna (see 4 ◉ Map p92, B3) has an unpretentious atmosphere; on weekends, '80s/'90s music videos are projected onto a huge screen. (It's al-

---

### Understand
**Prague's Grand Cafes**

Prague is known for pubs, Vienna for its coffee houses. Yet the Czech capital also boasts grand cafes that rival their Austrian cousins in looks (even if the actual coffee can't compete). At least the atmosphere is equivalent, and since the days of the Austro-Hungarian Empire onwards, Prague's ornate, high-ceilinged coffee houses have acted as public meeting spaces, hotbeds of political subversion and literary salons.

At various times Franz Kafka, robot 'creator' Karel Čapek and Albert Einstein all drank at Café Louvre, while across the road at Kavárna Slavia patrons included Milan Kundera, Václav Havel and other anticommunist dissidents.

### Understand
## Much Ado About Mucha

Alfons Mucha (1860–1939) is the Czech answer to Austria's Gustav Klimt, England's William Morris or Scotland's Charles Rennie Mackintosh. One of the fathers – if not *the* father – of the global art-nouveau movement, he found fame in Paris after producing a stunning poster for actress Sarah Bernhardt's 1895 play *Gismonda*.

A contract with Bernhardt, reams of advertising work and trips to America brought international renown. Mucha returned home in 1909, where he designed the banknotes for 1918's First Republic and produced his opus, a collection of huge canvases entitled *Slav Epic*.

Mucha created the stunning interiors of Prague's Municipal House and designed a beautiful stained-glass window for St Vitus Cathedral. His signature art-nouveau work is on display at the Mucha Museum (p93). Plans to relocate his *Slav Epic* paintings to Prague continue to be delayed with the lack of a suitable venue. Ask at the Mucha Museum for an update.

most impossible not to have fun when Madonna's *Like a Virgin* or Prince's *Kiss* is blasting throughout this cavernous space.) Brings in plenty of weekenders from the UK – who knew these tunes the first time around – and fresh-faced Erasmus students who didn't. Also hosts live music acts. (📞224 217 108; www.musicbar.cz; Lucerna pasáž, Štěpánská 61/Vodičkova 36; cover from 100Kč; ⏰8pm-4am; Ⓜ Můstek, 🚋3, 9, 14, 24 to Václavské náměstí, night tram 55, 56, 58)

## Entertainment

### Kino Světozor
CINEMA

12  Map p92, B3

Světozor is the only central Prague cinema for European art-house movies, cult documentaries and

mainstream and nonmainstream hits. Tucked away in yet another antique shopping arcade, it regularly shows Czech classics subtitled into English (noted by the 'English-friendly' label on the cinema's website listings) and participates in film festivals. Come early for a beer at the cinema bar, or feel free to take one into the movie with you. (📞224 946 824; www.kinos vetozor.cz; Vodičkova 41; tickets 80-110Kč; ⏰screenings from 11am; Ⓜ Můstek, 🚋3, 9, 14, 24 to Václavské náměstí)

### State Opera House
THEATRE

13  Map p92, D4

The State Opera's ballet troupe and opera ensemble are both well regarded internationally, and their Prague performances take place in this impressive neo-rococo building. An annual

Italian Opera Festival featuring Verdi and Puccini takes place in August and September. You can also book through Bohemia Ticket (www.bohemiaticket. cz). (Státní opera Praha; 📞224 227 266; www. opera.cz; Wilsonova 4; opera tickets 50-1150Kč, ballet tickets 100-800Kč; ⏲box office 10am-5.30pm Mon-Fri, 10am-noon & 1-5.30pm Sat & Sun; Ⓜ Muzeum)

# Shopping

### Bat'a
SHOES

**14** 🔒 Map p92, B2

For generations, schoolchildren the world over have known Bata shoes (called Bat'a in the original). However,

### Local Life
## Na příkopě

Intersecting Wenceslas Sq, and tracing the route that once ran around the Old Town, Na příkopě is one of Prague's most typical and reasonably fruitful shopping precincts.

In the 19th century this fashion-able street was the haunt of Austro-Hungarian cafe society. Today it's lined with all the usual high-street suspects – Benetton, H&M, Mango and Zara – and dotted with the huge shopping malls that charac-terise the Prague retail experience, including dům U černé růže (House of the Black Rose) at No 12, Mys-lbek pasáž (www.myslbek.com) at No 21 and Slovanský dům at No 22.

the Czech corporation's Wenceslas Sq store is a slightly more fashion-able experience, incorporating cool streetwear brands alongside its own over six retail floors. A great Czech success story, the family-run firm has been going since 1894, and this 1929 flagship store is considered a functionalist architectural master-piece. (www.bata.com; Václavské náměstí 6; Ⓜ Můstek)

### Artefakt
ARTS & CRAFTS

**15** 🔒 Map p92, B4

This funky little design shop looks like it should be attached to an art museum. Pop in to peruse the unique collection of jewellery, desktop sculp-tures, miniature paintings, ceramics and homewares – the place is great for gifts. (Štěpánská 53; Ⓜ Muzeum)

### Museum of Communism Gift Shop
BOOKS

**16** 🔒 Map p92, B1

While the museum itself leaves some-thing to be desired, the tongue-in-cheek gift shop is a fun place to poke around for an unusual souvenir – think Soviet-themed T-shirts, stickers, postcards and vintage posters. (Muzeum komunismu; www.muzeumkomunismu.cz; Na příkopě 10; Ⓜ Můstek)

### Moser
GLASSWARE

**17** 🔒 Map p92, B1

This exclusive Bohemian glassmaking company was founded in Karlovy Vary in 1857 and is famous for its ornate

Wenceslas Sq market at Christmas

designs, and equally over-the-top Gothic store design. For those preferring cleaner lines, one classic Moser design is Royal 9000, used in Prague Castle and the UN headquarters in New York. Only slightly less functional is Ivana Houserová's stunning candlestick – yours for 285,000Kč. Start saving. (www.moser-glass.com; dům U černé růže, Na příkopě 12; **M**Můstek)

## Palác Knih Neo Luxor BOOKS
**18** 🔒 Map p92, C3

Central Europe's largest bookshop is worth a browse, particularly for the wide basement selection of fiction and nonfiction in English, German, French and Russian, including Czech authors in translation. (www.neoluxor.cz; Václavské náměstí 41; **M**Muzeum)

## Promod FASHION
**19** 🔒 Map p92, B2

Continental, Asian and Middle Eastern readers, look away now; you'll be used to the delights this trendy young Gallic chain brings. However, American, Australasian, British and Latin American travellers will find this Czech branch a boon. Its range of affordable, covetable, up-to-the-minute fashion and jewellery might also be disposable, but it's a nice change from H&M. (www.promod.com; Václavské náměstí 772/2; **M**Můstek)

Explore

# Nové Město

Prague tour guides love to titillate their non-European customers with the fact that the city's Nové Město, or 'New' Town, was founded as long ago as 1348. Holy Roman Emperor Charles IV ordered it built to help transform his chosen imperial capital and, rather less grandly, because he fretted about fire risks and hygiene in cramped Staré Město.

RICHARD NEBESKY/LONELY PLANET IMAGES © ARCHITECT FRANK GEHRY

# The Sights in a Day

☀ Start your day with coffee, Viennese cake and spectacular views of Prague Castle at one of **Kavárna Slavia's** (p105) coveted window tables. Then wander over to **Slav Island** (p103) and, if the weather's nice, hire a rowboat for a lazy river ride – again with superb views of the castle and Charles Bridge. After docking, walk along the river towards architectural landmark the **Dancing Building** (pictured left; p103). If you're in the mood to splurge, sit down at **Céleste** (p103), the elegant restaurant on the famous building's 7th floor.

☼ Explore the quiet backstreets of so-called **SoNa** (p106), stopping for lemonade at **Kavárna Vojtěcha** (p106), a traditional Czech lunch at **Restaurace U Šumavy** (p104), or a wine flight at **Bokovka** (p104). Pop into the **Globe** (p103) to check out English translations of Czech novels.

☽ Get tickets to see the ballet or opera at the beautiful **National Theatre** (p106) or a jazz set at **Reduta Jazz Club** (p107). Before the show, admire sunset views from the riverbank, then stop into the Parisian-style **Café Louvre** (p105) for a cappuccino or a glass of wine.

For a local's walk in Nové Město, see p106.

 **Best of Nové Město**

**Bars & Pubs**
Bokovka (p104)

Café Louvre (p105)

**Food**
Céleste (p103)

Restaurace U Šumavy (p104)

**History**
Orthodox Cathedral of SS Cyril & Methodius (p103)

**Architecture**
Dancing Building (p103)

**Culture**
National Theatre (p106)

Reduta Jazz Club (p107)

Laterna Magika (p107)

## Getting There

Ⓜ **Metro** Line B to Karlovo Náměstí

Ⓜ **Metro** Line C to IP Pavlova

🚊 **Tram** Trams 4, 6, 10, 16, 22 to IP Pavlova or Karlovo Náměstí, or 9, 17, 18, 21, 22 to Národní divadlo

200 m
0.1 miles

**For reviews see**
- **◎** Sights — p103
- **◎** Eating — p103
- **◎** Drinking — p106
- **◎** Entertainment — p106
- **◎** Shopping — p107

Muzeum Ⓜ

Mezibranská

Krakovská

Ve Smečkách

Wenceslas Square (Václavské náměstí)

Štěpánská

Můstek Ⓜ

Ječná

V Jámě

Vodičkova

Školská

Na Rybníčku II

Franciscan Garden (Františkánská zahrada)

Palackého

Jungmannovo náměstí

Řeznická

Navrátilova

Lipová

Jungmannova

Vladislavova

Můstek Ⓜ

Purkyňova

Spálená

Lazarská

Malá Štěpánská

Žitná

Příčná

◎ 6
◎ 11

Národní Třída Ⓜ

◎ 15

Na Perštýně

Mikulandská

Ostrovní

◎ 8
13

Černá

Odborů

Charles Square (Karlovo náměstí)

Karlovo Náměstí Ⓜ

Národní třída

Batoliělská

Konviktská

Voršilská

V Jirchářích

Opatovická

Křemencová

Myslíkova

Orthodox Cathedral of SS Cyril & Methodius

Na Zderaze

NOVÉ MĚSTO

◎ 7
◎ 4

NOVÉ MĚSTO

Vyšehradská

Charles Square (Karlovo náměstí)

Václavská

◎ 14

Pštrossova

Nástruže

◎ 10

Šítků

Vojtěšská

◎ 5

Resslova

Václavská

Dittrichova

Divadelní

Smetanovo nábřeží

◎ 9
◎ 12

Masarykovo nábřeží

Slav Island (Slovanský ostrov)

◎ 3
Slav Island

Jirásek Square (Jiráskovo náměstí)

◎ 2

◎ 1

Jirásek Bridge (Jiráskův most)

Dancing Building

IP Pavlova Ⓜ

Kateřinská

# Sights

## Dancing Building
NOTABLE BUILDING

1 ⊙ Map p102, A4

Stroll along the riverfront to the gracefully twisting 'Dancing Building' by Bilbão Guggenheim creator Frank Gehry and local architect Vlado Milunič. Nicknamed the 'Fred & Ginger Building', this 1996 office is nipped in at the 'waist', to preserve neighbours' views, and has a top-floor restaurant, Céleste. Nearby, humble Rašínovo nábřeží 78 is what Václav Havel initially chose over Prague Castle as his presidential residence in 1989. (Tančící dům; Rašínovo nábřeží 80; Ⓜ Karlovo Náměstí, 🚊 17, 21 to Jiráskovo náměstí)

## Orthodox Cathedral of SS Cyril & Methodius
CHURCH

2 ⊙ Map p102, B4

In 1942 seven Czech partisans involved in assassinating Reichsprotektor Reinhard Heydrich took refuge from the Nazis in this cathedral. Their tale is legendary (see the boxed text, p105) and it's incredibly moving visiting the wreath-bedecked crypt where they resisted attempts to smoke and flood them out and then were either killed or took their own lives. Among multilingual explanations and bullet and shrapnel holes, you can see the Czechs' last desperate efforts to dig an escape route. (Kostel sv Cyril a Metodě; Resslova 9, entrance on Na Zderaze; adult/child 60/30Kč; ⊙10am-5pm Tue-Sun Mar-Oct, to 4pm Tue-Sun Nov-Feb; Ⓜ Karlovo Náměstí)

## Slav Island
ISLAND

3 ⊙ Map p102, A3

If you simply must take to the Vltava River, you'll probably find it more fun to do so under your own steam, in a small boat, rather than on a larger cruise. Several places have rowboats, but on this leafy island you'll find both rowboats (100Kč per half hour) and pedalos (150Kč per half hour) for hire between April and October (depending on weather). No reservations are taken, but you'll need to present your passport or similar ID. (Slovanský ostrov; Masarykovo nábřeží; 🚊6, 9,17, 18, 21, 22 to Národní divadlo)

# Eating

## Céleste
FRENCH €€€

On the 7th floor of the Dancing Building (see 1 ⊙ Map p102, A4). Expect a high standard of cuisine, decor and service – all with an innovative French tinge – plus the romance, grandeur and drama of Prague Castle just across the river. (☎221 984 160; www.celesterestaurant.cz; Rašínovo nábřeží 80; mains 425-755Kč; Ⓜ Karlovo Náměstí, 🚊17, 21 to Jiráskovo náměstí)

## Globe Bookstore & Café
CAFE €

4 🍴 Map p102, B3

This long-standing expat institution is an airy cafe, an English-language bookshop, a place to watch Wimbledon or the World Cup, or to have a leisurely weekend brunch, a bagel sandwich or

JEAN-PIERRE LESCOURRET/CORBIS ©

Café Louvre

a classic burger. The weekday happy hour (5pm to 7pm) is popular and the community noticeboard is a great asset for Prague newbies. (www.globebookstore .cz; Pštrossova 6; mains 145-295Kč; M Karlovo Náměstí;  )

### Klub Cestovatelu    MIDDLE EASTERN €

5  Map p102, A3

Lebanese flavours dominate at this relaxed part ethnic eatery and part travellers cafe, but the menu also touches down in India. There's a whole stack of travel magazines to get you planning your next trip, hookahs, belly dancers on Thursday nights and an ever-changing array of large-format travel photography on the walls. (www .hedvabnastezka.cz; Masarykovo nábřeží 22; mains 90-140; 17, 21; )

### Restaurace U Šumavy    CZECH €

6  Map p102, D4

Here's tasty proof that good-value Bohemian food still exists in central Prague. Ensconced in country-cottage decor, canny locals crowd in for lunch specials that remind them of their grandmother's cooking. The roast duck's good, and it's always worth taking a chance on the daily soup *(polévka)* special. (Štěpánská 3; mains 120-190Kč; M IP Pavlova)

## Drinking

### Bokovka    BAR

7  Map p102, B3

This compact wine bar is named after the movie *Sideways* (*Bokovka* in Czech), and is owned by filmmaking wine lovers. Wines include a great selection of excellent Moravian vintages, and good-value food platters are perfect for two or more. (www.bokovka.com; Pštrossova 8; Ⓜ Karlovo Náměstí)

### Café Louvre

CAFE

8 🍷 Map p102, B1

Others are more famous, but French-style Louvre is arguably Prague's most amenable grand cafe. The atmosphere is wonderfully old-world, but there's a proper nonsmoking section among its warren of red-walled rooms. Lovely any time of day – pop in for a great

breakfast before 11am, have lunch on the small garden patio, or play billiards and drink wine at night. (www.cafelouvre.cz; 1st fl, Národní třída 2; Ⓜ Národní Třída; )

### Kavárna Slavia

CAFE

9 🍷 Map p102, A1

The one-time hangout of Václav Havel and fellow anticommunist dissidents, and before them writers Rainer Maria Rilke and Franz Kafka, the Slavia now attracts locals and tourists equally. The revamped cherrywood and onyx interior and the forgettable food

---

### Understand

#### Seven Men at Daybreak

During his short reign as the Nazi Reichsprotektor for Bohemia and Moravia, SS general Reinhard Heydrich earned himself the epithet 'the butcher of Prague'. He arrived in the Czech capital a chief architect of the Holocaust and Hitler's heir apparent, and consolidated his reputation for arrogance by riding around the occupied city in an open-top Mercedes.

But installed in Czechoslovakia in 1941, the blond, steely-blue-eyed Heydrich was dead by mid-1942, killed by resistance fighters trained in Britain.

The daring 'Operation Anthropoid' almost didn't succeed. When Jozef Gabčík stepped in front of Heydrich's slow-moving car on 27 May, his gun jammed. However, his compatriot Jan Kubiš lobbed a grenade, from which the German later died.

The assassins and five accomplices fled but were betrayed in their hiding place at SS Cyril & Methodius (p103), where 750 German troops arrived at dawn on 18 June. In the ensuing six-hour siege, three of the Czechs were killed and four committed suicide rather than surrender. In retribution for Heydrich's death, the Nazis unleashed a wave of terror, even razing the village of Lidice (since rebuilt).

For more, see Callum MacDonald's *The Killing of Reinhard Heydrich* (on sale in the cathedral), Alan Burgess's *Seven Men at Daybreak* or the 1975 film *Operation Daybreak*.

aren't the reasons to come, however – just score a front table offering gorgeous views of the castle, then order some cake and coffee, and you won't want to leave. (www.cafeslavia.cz; Národní třída 1; ⏰8am-11pm; Ⓜ Národní Třída)

### Kavárna Vojtěcha
CAFE

10  Map p102, A3

This adorable but under-the-radar cafe, located on a quiet square near the Vltava, offers homemade lemon-

### Local Life
### Scouting Out SoNa

No one in Prague still uses the term 'SoNa' without irony, but the abbreviation coined by an American expat for the area south of Národní – and even leapt upon by *Wallpaper\** magazine as one of the world's 'hot 'hoods' – has stuck as a tongue-in-cheek description. The neighbourhood's quiet backstreets, lined with lesser-known ethnic eateries and student-populated cafes, are lovely to wander along as night falls.

**Lemon Leaf** (Map p102, A3; www.lemon.cz; Na Zderaze 14; mains 170-220Kč; 🌱) One of the city's better Thai restaurants does tasty curries and several good vegetarian dishes.

**Velbyra** (Map p102, A3; www.kavarnavelryba.cz; Opatovická 24; mains 90-130Kč; 🌱) Arty (and smoky) student cafe with a bohemian air, on-site art gallery and vegetarian-friendly snacks.

ade, well-prepared mojitos and large panels that open in warm weather, bathing many of the wooden tables in sunshine. (www.uvojtecha.cz; Vojtěšská 14; Ⓜ Národní Třída)

### Pivovarský Dům
PUB

11 🚇 Map p102, D4

Decked out with copper vats and tiled floors, this microbrewery isn't particularly Czech, although many locals do take refuge here. The main attraction is the flavoured beers; it may not sound appetising, but get adventurous and try the banana (the nicest), coffee or blueberry versions. Otherwise, stick to the house lager. (cnr Ječná & Lipová; 🚋4, 6, 10, 16, 22, 23 to Štěpánská)

## Entertainment

### National Theatre
THEATRE

12 ⭐ Map p102, A2

Notable for its ornate golden roof, the National Theatre was erected in the late 19th century as part of the Czech National Revival of culture. Despite sackings and administrative upheavals, it has preserved its excellent reputation for drama, opera and ballet. English subtitles are provided for operas but not for plays. Many of the ballet performances are staged in the allied Estates Theatre. (Národní divadlo; 📞info 224 901 448, tickets 224 901 377; www.narodni-divadlo.cz; Národní třída 2; tickets 100-1200Kč; ⏰box office 10am-6pm; Ⓜ Národní Třída)

## Reduta Jazz Club
CLUB

13 ⭐ Map p102, B1

Prague's oldest jazz club was founded in 1958 during the communist era, but is best known as the venue where US president Bill Clinton played the saxophone in 1994. It has an intimate setting, with smartly dressed patrons squeezing into tiered seats and lounges to soak up the big-band, swing and dixieland atmosphere. You can also book ahead through www.ticketpro.cz. (☎ 224 933 487; www.redutajazzclub.cz; Národní třída 20; cover varies; ⏱ box office from 3pm Mon-Fri, from 7pm Sat & Sun, venue 9pm-3am; Ⓜ Národní Trída, night tram 53, 57, 58, 59)

## Laterna Magika
THEATRE

14 ⭐ Map p102, A2

A unique style of nonverbal performance combining dance, music, film and light, Laterna Magika is a much-touted part of the national heritage developed in the late 1950s. The Black Light performances like *Casanova* and *Legend of the Argonauts* are fairly kitsch – they're best appreciated with an extremely camp sense of humour. The theatre is an interesting socialist relic at least. (☎ 224 931 482; www.laterna.cz; Nova Scéna theatre, Národní třída 4; tickets 210-680Kč; ⏱ box office 10am-8pm Mon-Sat; Ⓜ Národní Trída)

National Theatre balcony

# Shopping

## Tesco
DEPARTMENT STORE

15 🔒 Map p102, C1

Right above the metro, this five-storey monolith is no mere retail outlet. Oh no. It's a cultural phenomenon, too, as all Prague expat life seems to sashay down its aisles at some point. Indeed, they all seem to be milling around the basement supermarket – together – whenever you have to dash for a few late-night supplies. Stop here to pick up Becherovka, chocolate or other gift items. (www.tesco.com; Národní třída 26; Ⓜ Národní Trída)

# Local Life
# Vyšehrad, Prague's Other Castle

## Getting There

Vyšehrad is located on the banks of the Vltava River, just upstream from Nové Město.

Ⓜ **Metro** Line C to Vyšehrad

🚋 **Tram** Lines 7, 18, 24 to Ostrčilovo náměstí

For a few golden decades in the 11th century, Vyšehrad ('Castle on the Heights') was Prague's stronghold. Remnants of a castle, plus a 10th-century church and fortification, still grace the picturesque cliffs. Quiet, green and just slightly out of the way, today's Vyšehrad offers a stunning back-door view of Prague from the ruined citadel's magnificent ramparts. Visit www.praha-vysehrad.cz for more.

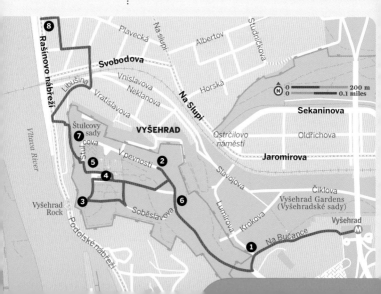

## ❶ Through the Old Gates

Heading away from the Vyšehrad metro station, you'll pass **Tábor Gate** and the remains of the Gothic **Špička Gate** before walking by the **house of Popelka Biliánová**, a 19th-century writer who wrote extensively on the legends of Vyšehrad.

## ❷ Into the Fortress

Through the **Brick Gate** the **Vyšehrad Casemates** (V pevnosti 5; adult/concession 30/20Kč; ◷9:30am-5pm) are the hidden passages and vaults that were used for imprisonment, defence, and storing weapons and ammunition. Included in the casemates are the underground Gorlice Hall, which now holds Charles Bridge's original statues, and various art and history exhibition spaces.

## ❸ Underground History

The atmospheric **Gothic Cellar** (admission 40Kč; ◷9:30am-5pm) houses a worthwhile exhibit, 'the Historic Faces of Vyšehrad,' that offers an overview of the history of Prague's fortification. A quick walk-through helps put Vyšehrad's sights into perspective.

## ❹ Last Church Standing

The 11th-century neo-Gothic **Church of SS Peter & Paul** (Kostel sv Petra a Pavla; K rotundě 10; adult/child 10/5Kč; ◷9am-noon & 1-5pm Wed-Mon) was one of the only structures in Vyšehrad that wasn't obliterated in 1420 during the 'battle of Vyšehrad'. After popping inside, walk around the pretty surrounding gardens and take in views over the Vltava.

## ❺ Mucha's Final Resting Place

The scenic **Vyšehrad Cemetery** (Vyšehradský hřbitov; ◷8am-5pm) is the final resting place of important Czech artists, writers and scholars. Composer Antonin Dvořák's grave is marked with a glittery mosaic inscription, while art-nouveau master Alfons Mucha is buried beneath the famous steel Slavín monument.

## ❻ Beer with a View

Just outside the castle ruins, **Hospudka Na Hradbach** (V pevnosti 144) is an outdoor beer garden with fantastic views over the city. Come for Pilsner Urquell and a grilled sausage or chicken sandwich with a young, mostly local crowd.

## ❼ Outdoor Entertainment

If you're visiting during the warmer months, look out for musical performances and shows, which include an annual Shakespeare festival, at Vyšehrad's **Open-Air Theatre** (Letní Scéna Vyšehrad; www.studiodva.cz/vysehrad; ticket prices vary).

## ❽ Dinner off the Beaten Path

On your way out of Vyšehrad, stop for a meal at **Oliva** (www.olivarestaurant.cz; Plavecká 4; mains 135-425Kč; ◫3, 7, 16, 17, 21 to Výtoň; ◷▯), a classy Mediterranean restaurant with a menu of delicious dishes prepared with fresh ingredients, including Tunisian-style octopus, grilled tuna steaks and lemon tart with lime sorbet.

Explore

# Vinohrady & Žižkov

Vinohrady and Žižkov are the yin and yang of residential Prague. Gentrified Vinohrady, named for its days as Emperor Charles IV's vineyards, still boasts high-ceilinged, art-nouveau apartment buildings and is popular with arty foreign expats. The 'people's republic' of Žižkov is historically working class, rebellious and revolutionary, famed for its numerous pubs, alternative nightlife, TV tower and multiethnicity.

# The Sights in a Day

 Start your day with a cappuccino and homemade pastries at cool **Café Pavlač** (p119). Then walk uphill towards Jiřiho z Podebrad, stopping into the **Church of the Most Sacred Heart of Our Lord** (p116), the huge church right on the square. Continue onto the **Jewish Cemetery** (p116) to see the final resting place of Franz Kafka.

 Head back towards **Žižkov Tower** (pictured left; p116), eyeing up the larger-than-life baby statues as you approach, then ascending the observation tower for views. Then have a leisurely lunch at culinary standout **Mozaika** (p118). If you're craving a rest on a park bench, walk over to leafy **Riegrovy sady** (p117), where locals congregate for picnics, afternoon siestas, leisurely strolls and beer drinking.

☾ After an elegant dinner at Italian restaurant **Aromi** (p118) or more down-to-earth Czech fare at **Pastička** (p118), check out some of the neighbourhood's popular watering holes. Finish the day at a slick nightclub like **Infinity** (p119), or, depending on what's on the schedule, catch some live music at **Palác Akropolis** (p121) or **Radost FX** (p119).

For a local's drinking tour of Vinohrady & Žižkov, see p112.

## ○ Local Life

Drinking tour of Vinohrady & Žižkov (p112)

## ♥ Best of Prague

**Bars & Pubs**

Riegrovy Sady Park Café (p112)

Kaaba (p113)

Hapu (p113)

**History**

Žižkov Tower (p116)

**Nightlife**

Infinity (p119)

Palác Akropolis (p121)

Radost FX (p119)

**Gay & Lesbian**

Termix (p120)

Club ON (p120)

Saints (p119)

## Getting There

Ⓜ **Metro** Line A to Náměstí Míru, Jiřiho z Podebrad or Flora

🚋 **Tram** Lines 10, 11, 16, 19, 26 to Náměstí Míru or Jiřiho z Podebrad

## Local Life
# Drinking Tour of Vinohrady & Žižkov

In the city of Prague, there's no better place to make a night of it: Žižkov, on one side, proudly claims to have more pubs per square metre than anywhere else in the world, while on the other side, classy Vinohrady is home to some serious wine bars and cocktail bars where the staff know how to mix a drink.

**❶ Riegrovy Sady Beer Garden**
Start the night off in an outdoor venue: before you even see it, you'll probably hear the heavy chink of glasses rumbling out from under the trees at **Riegrovy Sady Park Café** (Riegrovy sady; ⏱ depending on weather, at least Apr-Oct; Ⓜ Náměstí Míru, 🚊 11 to Italská, night tram 55, 58), a huge German-style beer garden. Inside, hundreds of locals (and their dogs) are making merry with cheap Gambrinus.

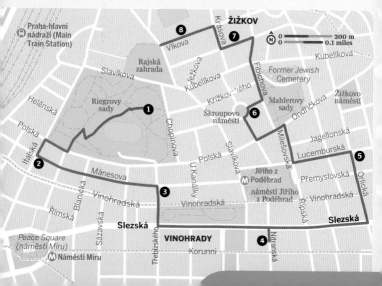

### ❷ Czech Wine at Kaaba

Stylish **Kaaba** (www.kaaba.cz; Mánesova 20; 🚇11 to Italská, night tram 55, 58) flaunts retro furniture and pastel-coloured decor that could have come straight from the award-winning Czech pavilion at the 1958 Brussels Expo. Gourmet imported coffee (including Jamaican Blue Mountain), snacks and an extensive list of Czech and imported wines are served.

### ❸ Classy Cocktails at Bar & Books

Continue onto another of Vinohrady's sophisticated drinking dens, **Bar & Books** (www.barandbooks.cz/manesova; Mánesova 64; Ⓜ Jiřího z Poděbrad, night tram 55, 58). The sensuous cocktail lounge features lush library-themed decor, top-shelf liquor and live music on Wednesday nights. It's a place suited for a predinner aperitif with friends or a romantic late-night rendezvous.

### ❹ Underground Drinking at Sudička

Descend the stairs into a more down-to-earth drinking den, the subterranean **Sudička** (www.sudicka.cz; Nitranská 7; Ⓜ Jiřího z Poděbrad, night tram 55, 58). After dark, local 20- and 30-somethings drink beer and inexpensive carafes of house wine in the candlelit rustic space.

### ❺ Cocktails at Hapu

This place mixes a mean cocktail – arguably the best in town – with freshly squeezed fruit juices. Stopping at tiny **Hapu** (Orlická 8; Ⓜ Jiřího z Poděbrad, night tram 51, 57, 59) is like popping around for a drink in a popular friend's living room – if you happen to have a friend with an incredibly well-stocked bar, that is.

### ❻ Beer at U Sadu

The congenial neighbourhood pub **U Sadu** (www.usadu.cz; Škroupovo náměstí; Ⓜ Jiřího z Poděbrad, night tram 51, 57, 59) is supremely popular with old locals, dreadlocked students and expats alike. Later at night, the breezy outdoor tables close for business and everyone moves into the smoky basement bar.

### ❼ Nightcap at Bukowski's

On the Žižkov street that's reckoned to have more drinking dens per metre than anywhere else in Prague, **Bukowski's Bar** (Bořivojova 86; 🚋 5, 9, 26 to Husinecká, night tram 55, 58) is a cut above its neighbours. It's named after the hard-drinking American poet Charles Bukowski – expect cool tunes and confident cocktails.

### ❽ Late Night at the Seven Wolves

Dance the night away at **Sedm Vlků** (www.sedmvlku.cz; Vlkova 7; 🚋 5, 9, 26, night tram 55, 58). 'Seven Wolves' is a cool, two-level, art-studenty cafe-bar and club where DJs pump out techno, breakbeat and drum'n'bass in the darkened cellar from 9pm on Friday and Saturday nights.

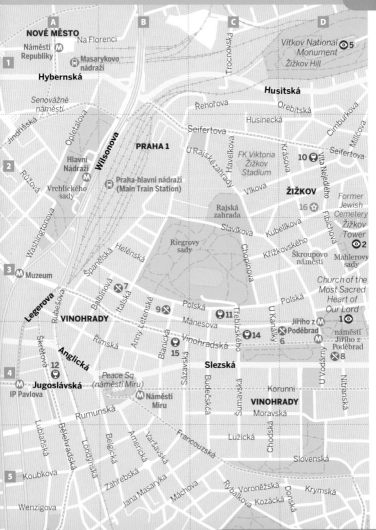

**A**  **B**  **C**  **D**

NOVÉ MĚSTO

Náměstí Ⓜ
Republiky

Na Florenci

Ⓜ Masarykovo
nádraží

Trocnovská

Vítkov National Ⓞ5
Monument
Žižkov Hill

**1**

Hybernská

Husitská

Senovážné
náměstí

Řehořova

Orebitská

Jindřišská

Opletalova

Husinecká

Cimburkova

Wilsonova

Seifertova

Millcova

PRAHA 1

U Rajské zahrady

FK Viktoria
Žižkov
Stadium

Havelkova

Krásová

Seifertova

10 Ⓠ

Vita Nejedlého

Hlavní
Nádraží

**2**

Růžová

Praha-hlavní nádraží
(Main Train Station)

Vlkova

ŽIŽKOV

Vrchlického
sady

Rajská
zahrada

16 ☆

Former
Jewish
Cemetery

Washingtonova

Slavíkova

Kubelíkova

Fibichova

Žižkov
Tower

Riegrovy
sady

Chopinova

Křížkovského

Škroupovo
náměstí

Ⓞ2

Ⓜ Muzeum

**3**

Helénská

Španělská

Mahlerovy
sady

Church of the
Most Sacred
Heart of
Our Lord

Legerova

Rubešova

Balbínova

Italská

Ⓧ7

Ⓧ9

Polská

Ⓠ11

Polská

Jiřího z Ⓜ
Poděbrad

1 Ⓞ

VINOHRADY

Římská

Anny Letenské

Mánesova

Třebízského

U kanálky

6

náměstí
Jiřího z
Poděbrad

Ⓧ8

Škrétova

Anglická

Blanická

Vinohradská

Ⓠ14

U Vodárny

Nitranská

15 Ⓠ

Sázavská

Slezská

12 Ⓠ

Ⓜ
Jugoslávská

Peace Sq
(náměstí Míru)

Budečská

Šumavská

Korunni

**4**

IP Pavlova

Rumunská

Ⓜ Náměstí
Míru

VINOHRADY
Moravská

Lublaňská

Bělehradská

Belgická

Americká

Varšavská

Francouzská

Lužická

Chodská

Slovenská

**5**

Koubkova

Londýnská

Záhřebská

Jana Masaryka

Máchova

Rybalkova

Voroněžská

Kozácká

Donská

Krymská

Wenzigova

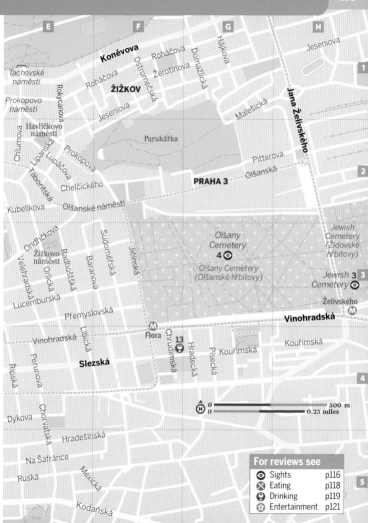

# Sights

### Church of the Most Sacred Heart of Our Lord CHURCH

1 Map p114, D3

In the green square above Jiřího z Poděbrad metro stands one of Europe's great modern churches. Square-angled and blocky, the unusual Sacred Heart (1932) merges classical Greek and cubist influences, and is also inspired by Egyptian temples and early Christian basilicas. Its facade is glazed brown brick, while its massive tombstonelike bell tower features an enormous see-through clock. The church is the work of Jože Plečnik, the Slovenian architect who revamped Prague Castle in the early 20th century. (Kostel Nejsvětějšího Srdce Páně; náměstí Jiřího z Poděbrad 19; M Jiřího z Poděbrad)

### Žižkov Tower MONUMENT

2 Map p114, D3

Hideous or futuristic? *Miminka,* the 10 giant babies crawling up Prague's TV transmitter, has quelled debates about this structure (1985–92), as people just enjoy the quirkiness that sculptor David Černý has brought to the city's tallest landmark. Attractively lighting the 216m needle at night helps, too. High-speed lifts go to a 93m observation deck, but many people prefer the view from Petřín Lookout Tower. (Žižkovská věž; www.praguerocket .com; Mahlerovy sady 1; adult/child 150/60Kč; ⏲10am-10pm; M Jiřího z Poděbrad)

### Jewish Cemetery HISTORIC SITE

3 Map p114, H3

The grave of Franz Kafka (1883–1924) is the most visited in this leafy cemetery. The writer lies buried with his parents opposite a plaque for his friend Max Brod; turn right at row 21, then left at the wall until you come to the end of the sector. Fans commemorate Kafka's death on 3 June. (Židovské hřbitovy; Izraelská 1; admission free; ⏲9am-5pm Sun-Thu, to 2pm Fri Apr-Oct, 9am-4pm Sun-Thu, to 2pm Fri Nov-Mar, last entry 30min before closing, closed Jewish holidays; M Želivského)

---

### Understand

## How the Tower Got Its Babies

Žižkov Tower first acquired its babies in 2000 as an art installation during Prague's reign as a European City of Culture. They came down at the end of that tenure, but the resulting public outcry meant they were reinstated, and it appears they're now a permanent fixture.

Meanwhile, creator David Černý continues to court controversy. In 2006 his sculpture of Saddam Hussein in a giant fish tank was temporarily banned in Belgium and Poland, and his *Entropa* installation upset the EU in 2009. His latest project is the sprawling MeetFactory, offering space to visiting artists in the grimier depths of Smíchov.

Church of the Most Sacred Heart of Our Lord

### Olšany Cemetery
HISTORIC SITE

4 ◉ Map p114, G3

Prague's atmospheric main burial ground was founded in 1680 but is best known for a relatively recent grave. Jan Palach, the student who set himself on fire in 1969 in protest at the Soviet invasion (see p91), is buried 50m to the right of the main gate on Vinohradská. (Olšanské hřbitovy; Vinohradská 153; admission free; ⊗8am-7pm May-Sep, to 6pm Mar, Apr & Oct, 9am-4pm Nov-Feb; Ⓜ Flora)

### Vítkov National Monument
MONUMENT

5 ◉ Map p114, D1

This hilltop monument celebrates 15th-century Hussite independence fighter and commander Jan Žižka with a 9m equestrian statue of the one-eyed warrior after whom Žižkov is named. Great views. (Národní památník Vítkov; www.nm.cz; U památníku 1900; Ⓜ Florenc)

## ◉ Local Life
### Riegrovy Sady

The hilltop park **Riegrovy sady** (Riegrovy sady; Ⓜ Náměstí Míru, 🚊 11 to Italská) gets press for its popular beer garden (p112), but the green space itself is worthy of a visit: on sunny days, the grassy slopes face a magnificent view of Prague Castle and the city's red roofs. For a little peace and quiet, grab a beer or a sandwich from the beer garden (or a smaller cafe in the park) and park yourself on a wooden bench.

---

## Understand
### Absinth

- - - - - - - - - - - - - - - - - - - - - - - -

For many visitors, Prague is synonymous with absinth. That's been the case since the 1990s, when Czech drinks firm Hills cleverly revived this long-banned, legendary and allegedly hallucinatory 19th-century French-Swiss tipple. Today, however, the Swiss and French have resumed production of genuine *'fée verte',* and connoisseurs have become pretty sniffy about replica 'Czechsinths'.

What's the difference? Most Czech brands (whether spelt absinth or absinthe) use oil to mix the active ingredient, wormwood, into the liquid, instead of properly distilling it. If you'll be packing a bottle in your suitcase, try the pricey but excellent Czech Cami's Absinthe Toulouse Lautrec (about 1100Kč, usually at Tesco on Národní třída).

---

# Eating

### Aromi                                        ITALIAN €€€

6  Map p114, D4

This gourmet Italian restaurant, specialising in cuisine from the Marché region, enjoys an exulted reputation. With rustic exposed-brick walls and polished wooden tables set well apart, plus a central display of imported delicacies, the place is businesslike at lunch and romantic in the evenings. Choose between the renowned seafood or rarities like *vincisgrassi alla Marchigiana* (a rich lasagne). (www.aromi.cz; Mánesova 78; mains 295-495Kč; M Jiřího z Poděbrad; ✐)

### Masala                                       INDIAN €€

7  Map p114, B3

The relaxed, home-style Masala is popular with locals and expats for its tasty Indian cuisine. Decor and service is unpretentious, allowing the food to shine. The owners, on request, will add enough spicy heat to keep their well-travelled clientele satisfied. Forgo rice and mop up Masala's sauces with its excellent naan. (www.masala.cz; Mánesova 13; mains 159-279Kč; M Muzeum; ✐)

### Mozaika                                       INTERNATIONAL €€

8  Map p114, D4

Mozaika is one of Prague's shining lights due to its consistently excellent food. The contemporary bistro-style menu includes red snapper, home-made ravioli, Asian risotto, and Mozaika's famous (in Prague) burger. Rich desserts are best shared. (✆224 253 011; www.restaurantmozaika.cz; Nitranská 13; mains 180-330Kč; M Jiřího z Poděbrad; ✐)

### Pastička                                     CZECH, INTERNATIONAL €

9  Map p114, B3

Locals show up at the down-to-earth Irish-pub-style 'Mousetrap' for excellent Bernard beer, huge meaty meals, and to feel good about living in the funky part of town. Grab a table in the little garden and join them. (www.pasticka.cz; Blanická 24; mains 150-300Kč; Jiřího z Poděbrad)

# Drinking

### Café Pavlač
CAFE

**10** Map p114, D2

A funky, beautifully illuminated central bar is the centrepiece of this sleek but easygoing cafe. Come in the morning for a Viennese coffee and the newspaper, in the afternoon for a freshly squeezed elderberry lemonade, or at night for beer, Moravian wine or the famous Czech *slivovice* (plum brandy). (www.cafepavlac.cz; Víta Nejedlého 23; 5, 9, 26 to Husinecká; night tram 55, 58)

### Saints
BAR

**11** Map p114, C3

Sealing the deal on Prague's booming 'gay quarter' in Vinohrady, this British-run bar is laid-back, friendly and serves good drinks. With a multinational staff speaking many languages, for newcomers it's the perfect entrée to the local scene. (www.saintsbar.cz; Polská 32; Jiřího z Poděbrad, night tram 51, 57, 59)

### Radost FX
CLUB

**12** Map p114, A4

Another Prague stalwart, Radost is a high-profile, fairly mainstream club that pulls in big-name DJs. There's a

chilled-out, bohemian atmosphere, with Moroccan-boudoir-meets-Moulin-Rouge decor, and the upstairs lounge serves food late. Thursday's hip-hop night, FXbounce (www.fxbounce.com), is a weekly highlight. (www.radostfx.cz; Bělehradská 120; cover 100-300Kč; 10pm-6am; IP Pavlova, night tram 51, 56, 57, 59)

### Infinity
CLUB

**13** Map p114, F4

Smart-casual clubbing gear is the order of the day in this midsized cellar with exposed-brick walls and sophisticated lighting. Alternating between

---

#### Understand
#### Not Big in Belgium

Design buffs beware. When Czechs talk of the Brussels style, they're not referring to Belgian art nouveau or anything related to Henry Van de Velde. Rather, they're harking back to a heyday of their own national design when, despite the constraints of working under a communist regime, Czechoslovakia triumphed with its circular restaurant pavilion at the 1958 Brussels Expo. More than 100 local designers took away awards, including porcelain designer Jaroslav Ježek, who won the Grand Prix for his Elka coffee service.

The aesthetics of the time were similar to Kaaba's (p113). For a more authentic take, visit Veletržní Palace (p124).

upbeat happy house and nostalgic '60s to '90s nights, it's much more enjoyable than its reputation as the second-biggest pick-up joint in Prague might suggest. (We're not telling you the first!) Follow the crowds from nearby Flora metro station and down through the middle of the ground-floor restaurant. (www.infinitybar.cz; Chrudimská 2a/2526; ⏰6pm-3am Mon-Sat, to 1am Sun; Ⓜ Flora, night tram 51)

## Termix

CLUB

**14** 🚇 Map p114, C4

A local gay favourite, Termix is an industrial-looking bar (with a car sticking out of one wall) with a small-ish dance floor and dark room. The leading Wednesday night goes native with Czech pop tunes and is nick-named 'Hezky Cesky' after the cute Czech customers. (www.club-termix .cz; Trebízského 4a; admission free; ⏰9pm-5am Wed-Sun; Ⓜ Náměstí Míru or Jiřího z Poděbrad, night tram 51, 57, 59)

## Club ON

CLUB

**15** 🚇 Map p114, B4

Formerly known as Valentino, this is Prague's one true gay superclub, boasting three floors, two dance floors, four bars and two dark rooms. It's particularly packed and sweaty on the weekends. The music alternates

RICHARD NEBESKY/LONELY PLANET IMAGES ©

Kaaba (p113)

## Understand
### Ten Degrees

Beer drinking is practically a national sport in the Czech Republic. Visitors can get up to speed by learning a few quick facts. Following a 17th-century custom, Czech beer is measured in 'degrees'. However, although that degree sign has become interchangeable with a percentage sign recently, it's not the amount of alcohol it measures. Rather, the Czech degree represents the malt extract used during brewing and the alcohol percentage is less than half this. Roughly, a 10-degree Czech beer contains 4% alcohol; a 12-degree beer has 4.5% to 5%.

between cool house and cheesy Czech pop, depending where in the complex you drift. (www.onclub.cz; Vinohradská 40; cover charge varies, some nights free; ⏱5pm-5am; Ⓜ Náměstí Míru, night tram 51, 57, 59)

# Entertainment

### Palác Akropolis                    CLUB
16 ⭐ Map p114, D2

This huge Prague institution is a sticky-floored shrine to alternative music and drama with a broad cross-section of regulars. Its trump card is its innovative roster of gigs, which range from Boban Markovic to Sigur Ros to the Strokes. Otherwise, when the 850-capacity concert hall is shut and all you have is the speak-easy vibe in the two smaller DJ bars, the appeal of the place might be a bit difficult for newcomers to fathom. (📞296 330 911; www.palacakropolis.cz; Kubelíkova 27; cover free-150Kč; ⏱club 7pm-5am; 🚊5, 9, 26, night tram 51, 57, 59)

Explore

# Holešovice

In Holešovice, you start to appreciate Prague as a genuine work-ing city. Though sections of this former industrial quarter remain somewhat rundown, the neighbourhood has been slowly gentrifying. Locals flock to the hilltop beer garden and park to relax, walk their dogs, and take in sunset views; visitors come to see the impressive art galleries at Veletržní Palace.

# The Sights in a Day

Spend the morning taking in the Czech cubist works, plus art by Picasso, Monet, Rodin and Cezanne, at **Veletržní Palace** (pictured left; p124). Then stop into art-house cinema **Bio Oko** (p128) to see what's on, stopping at the bar for a coffee.

Catch tram 12 to the **DOX Centre for Contemporary Art** (p127) to survey the futuristic installations and supermodern Czech exhibitions. Don't miss a visit to the DOX Centre's inviting cafe. If you've had your fill of art, head for wide-open spaces – choose between the former royal playground of sprawling **Stromovka Park** (p128), or opt for lovely city views at **Letná Gardens & Terrace** (p127), not to mention one of the city's most famous beer gardens, **Letná Beer Garden** (p128). After a beer or two, head over to **Fraktal** (p127) for the famous house burger.

In the mood for a show? Try **Výstaviště** (p131) and a short performance by the Prague Ballet Theatre at **Křižíkova Fountain**. If you're up for clubbing, this is the neighbourhood to be in: you can make a night of it at funky, postindustrial **Cross Club** (p128), upscale 'superclubs' **Mecca** (p128) or **SaSaZu** (p129), or laid-back DJ lounge **Wakata** (p129).

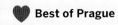

## ◉ Top Sights
Veletržní Palace (p124)

## ♥ Best of Prague

**Bars & Pubs**
Letná Beer Garden (p128)

Pivovar U Bulovky (p128)

**Art**
Veletržní Palace (p124)

DOX Centre for Contemporary Art (p127)

**For Kids**
Letná Gardens (p127)

Stromovka Park (p128)

Bio Oko (p128)

**Nightlife**
Mecca (p128)

SaSaZu (p129)

## Getting There

🚊 **Tram** Lines 1, 8, 15, 25, 26 to Letenské náměstí

🚊 **Tram** Lines 5, 12, 14, 17 to Výstaviště

Ⓜ **Metro** Line C to Nádraží Holešovice

## Top Sights
# Veletržní Palace

Don't let the name fool you: if you're wandering around Holešovice looking for a palace like others you've seen in Prague, you'll miss this modern museum altogether. The stunning functionalist building houses the National Gallery's jaw-dropping collection of 20th- and 21st-century Czech and European art. Look for Czech cubist masterpieces, French impressionist works, and pieces by big names like Klimt and Picasso, plus a striking exhibit on communist-era social realism. There's also a well-curated collection of photography, furniture, fashion and set design.

◉ Map p126, C3

www.ngprague.cz

Dukelských hrdinů 47

adult/concession 250/120Kč

⊙ 10am-6pm Tue-Sun

🚋 12, 14, 17 to Veletržní

National Gallery, Veletržní Palace

# Don't Miss

### Overview from the Elevator
Catch the all-glass lift from the Small Hall to get a quick overview of the atrium displays. Note the striking, spare, all-white colour scheme and the Central Hall's airy dimensions – before the palace housed an art collection, it was used as an exhibition space for industrial equipment.

### French Collection
Thanks to a strong Bohemian interest in French painting – and several generous donations – the palace's 3rd floor has an impressive collection of 19th- and 20th-century French art. Artists represented include Monet, Gauguin, Cézanne, Picasso, Delacroix and Rodin. Look for Gauguin's *Flight* and Van Gogh's *Green Wheat*.

### Avant-Garde Czech Art
Also on the 3rd floor, the museum's display of 20th-century national art is one of the country's finest. Standouts include the geometric works by Frantiek Kupka and cubist painting, ceramics and design by several different artists – these paintings show an interesting parallel with the concurrent art scene in Paris. On the 2nd floor, look for the most contemporary Czech works across several genres.

### Female Imagery in the International Collection
The 20th-century international collection, on the 1st floor, boasts works by some major names: Klimt, Schiele, Sherman and Miró, to name a few. Two highlights take on feminine themes: Klimt's luscious, vibrantly hued *The Virgins* and Schiele's much darker, foreboding *Pregnant Woman and Death*.

## ☑ Top Tips

▶ The museum is huge – it would be easy to spend an entire day here. If you only have an hour or two, just hit the highlights listed here.

▶ Museum admission is free from 3pm to 8pm on the first Wednesday of the month.

▶ If you're a couple travelling with children, the museum offers a family pass for the deeply discounted price of 350Kč.

▶ Pick up postcards or small souvenirs at the museum shop.

## ✗ Take a Break

The museum cafe, located on the ground floor and open during museum hours, is convenient for a coffee.

A few blocks away from the museum, the funky cafe at Bio Oko (p128) is a charming place to stop for a beer.

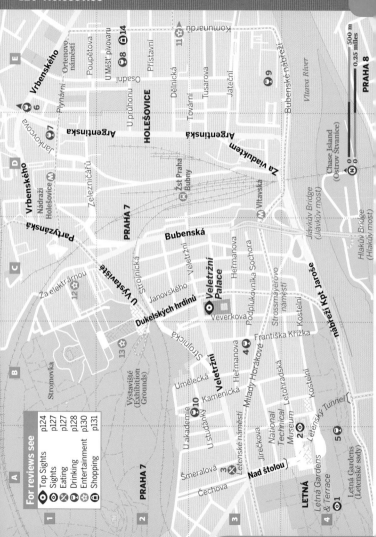

PRAHA 8
PRAHA 7

HOLEŠOVICE

Bubenská

LETNÁ
Letná Gardens & Terrace
Letná Gardens (Letenské sady)

# Sights

### Letná Gardens & Terrace    PARK

 **1** Map p126, A4

This vast park has great views and open spaces where kids can run and play. In the 1950s the world's largest statue of Stalin was built here, only to be blown up in 1962. You'll find skateboarders, a beer garden (see p128) and artist Vratislav Karel Novák's huge metronome symbolising the passage of time. Little ones can ride on Europe's oldest carousel. (Letenské sady; 🚋12, 17 to Čechův most)

### National Technical Museum    MUSEUM

 **2** Map p126, A4

Highly rated for its collection of vintage trains, planes and cars, including imperial Austro-Hungarian rail carriages, old Škoda and Tatra cars and Jawa motorcycles, this museum recently reopened after renovations. It features permanent exhibits on transport, architecture, design, astronomy and printing/photography. (Národní technické muzeum; 📞220 399 111; www.ntm.cz; Kostelní 42; adult/concession 170/90Kč; ⏱10am-6pm Tue-Sun; 🚋1, 8,15, 25, 26 to Letenské náměstí)

# Eating

### Fraktal    INTERNATIONAL €

 **3** Map p126, A3

This low-lit cellar feels like a genuine neighbourhood eatery and watering hole, with Czech and expat regulars treating the staff like old friends. Newcomers are made to feel welcome, too. Although the nightly focus is on beer (Pilsner Urquell, Gambrinus and Kozel), the food is well produced. Expats rave about its gourmet burgers; Mexican dishes, steaks, salads and excellent weekend brunches (11am to 3.30pm) are also on offer. (www.fraktalbar.cz; Šmeralová 1; mains 105-295Kč; 🚋1, 8, 15, 25, 26 to Letenské náměstí, night tram 51, 56; 🛜🍴)

## Local Life

## DOX Centre for Contemporary Art

The urban renewal of the working-class neighbourhood of Holešovice has been talked about for years. The 2008 opening of the impressive **DOX Centre for Contemporary Art** (Map p126, F1; DOX Centrum současného umění; 📞774 145 434; www.doxprague.org; Poupětova 1; ⏱10am-6pm Sat-Mon, 11am-7pm Wed-Fri; adult/concession 180/90Kč; 🚋5, 12, 15 to Ortoveno náměstí) could be a harbinger of things to come. The minimalist multilevel building occupies an entire corner block, providing Prague's most capacious gallery space, studded with a diverse range of thought-provoking contemporary art and photography. Don't miss DOX's excellent cafe and bookshop. Make an arty day of it and catch tram 12 to the nearby Veletržní Palace.

# Drinking

### Bio Oko                                    CAFE

4  Map p126, B3

Seek out the retro cafe in this art-house cinema, and imagine yourself back in the '50s. A location out of Prague's tourist buzz helps with thoroughly sensible pricing for excellent coffee, beer and cocktails. There are themed film series, children's events, free wi-fi, book exchanges – plenty of excuses to relax and have another drink. (www.biooko.net; Františka Křížka 15; 1, 8, 15, 25, 26; 🛜 👬)

### Letná Beer Garden          BEER GARDEN

5  Map p126, A4

Spread along a shaded landing at the eastern end of Letná Gardens, this slew of wooden tables provides one of the city's best views, looking across the river to the spires of Staré Město, and southwest to Malá Strana. You can rely on its being open June to September,

> **Local Life**
> ### Stromovka Park
> Prague's largest central park, **Stromovka** (Map p126, B1; www.stromovka .cz; 5, 12, 14, 15, 17 to Výstaviště) was a medieval hunting ground for royals; now it's popular with strollers, joggers, cyclists and inline skaters. Kids can climb on the huge gnarled branches of ancient fallen trees – and adults will appreciate the lavish tulip display in spring.

but you'll often find it serving up Gambrinus on sunny winter days, too. (Letná Gardens; 12, 17 to Čechův most)

### Pivovar U Bulovky             PUB

6  Map p126, E1

This unassuming suburban pub and microbrewery is a city legend. It's not just the range of award-winning beers, although these include a delicious house *ležak* (lager) as well as ales, stouts, Düsseldorf-style *Alts* and Bavarian-like *Weissbiers*. Part of the pub's appeal is its welcoming hum and local atmosphere. (www.pivovarubulovky.cz; Bulovka 17; 10, 15, 24, 25 to Bulovka)

### Cross Club                       CLUB

7  Map p126, D1

An eclectic program from drum and bass, jungle, dub and reggae to electro, techno and live music goes on in this bar, but the main attraction is the venue itself. Both the ground floor and basement of a rundown apartment block have been transformed into a work of industrial or sci-fi art, with glowing homemade lighting installations, kinetic sculptures formed from bits of junk metal, film reels, engine parts and even a bus outside. Alternative and unique. (www.crossclub.cz; Plynární 23; admission free-100Kč; ⏰4pm-late; 🅼Nádraží Holešovice, night tram 53, 54)

### Mecca                            CLUB

8  Map p126, E2

A slice of Ibiza in the suburbs, Mecca is a premier name on the clubbing

RICHARD NEBESKY/LONELY PLANET IMAGES ©

Letná Beer Garden

scene. Its black-walled interior is sultry, with the relatively small, DJ-dominated dance floor reached via a restaurant area popular with models, film stars and fashionistas, while there's a chill-out lounge with curvy couches downstairs. The midweek '80s/'90s night is more relaxed. (www.mecca.cz; U průhonu 3; cover charge varies; 🚋5, 12, 15 to U Průhonu, night tram 54)

## SaSaZu                                    CLUB
**9** 🚇 Map p126, E3

Only open since 2009, this self-proclaimed 'superclub' is situated in the Rivertown complex at Prague's riverside markets. If international DJs playing in a UFO-styled DJ booth, visiting hip-hop stars, and

phalanxes of leggy supermodels interest you, look no further. Those seeking a more subtle and surprising night out might find themselves lost and bewildered amid the lights and lasers. (www.sasazu.com; Bubenské nábřeží 306; admission varies by event; Ⓜ Vlatavská, 🚋1, 3, 15, 25 to Pražsak tržnice)

## Wakata                                    CLUB
**10** 🚇 Map p126, B3

There's no designer chic or style statements in this small, laid-back DJ lounge, full of colourful urban wall murals and some interestingly welded barstools. Enjoy inexpensive beers and cocktails as you bop along to a nightly soundtrack of funk, Latin, dub, ambient, jungle, reggae or hip-hop.

(www.wakata.eu; Malířská 14; admission free; 🚋1, 8, 15, 25, 26 to Letenské náměstí, night tram 51, 56)

# Entertainment

## O2 Arena
CONCERT HALL

11 ⭐ Map p126, E2

This 18,000-capacity venue has hosted gigs from Leonard Cohen and Coldplay to George Michael. It's also home to hockey team HC Slavia; the stadium was built to host the 2004 Ice Hockey World Championships. (📞266 121 111; www.o2arena.cz, www.hc-slavia .cz; Ocelářská 2; tickets 200-500Kč; Ⓜ Českomoravská)

## Tesla Arena
SPORTING ARENA

12 ⭐ Map p126, C1

Prague's other big ice hockey team, HC Sparta, plays at this 13,000-capacity arena. The 1960s stadium could do with a major overhaul, but by the sharp end of the season (February and March) it's filled with the Sparta faithful watching the fastest show in town. Most of the big Czech stars ply their trade in North America's National Hockey League, but if you're a *hokej* newbie, you'll still be dazzled by the skills on display locally. (📞266 727 443; www.hcsparta.cz, www.ticket portal.cz; Tesla Arena, Za elektrárnou 419; tickets 120-400Kč; Ⓜ Nádraží Holešovice, 🚋5, 12, 14, 15, 17 to Výstaviště)

O2 Arena

## Understand

### Oh, How We Laughed at Škoda...

During the communist era, Czechoslovakia's less-than-perfect Škoda car became the butt of much the same jokes as East Germany's Trabant – although the Škoda was more ridiculed abroad than at home. Indeed, when Volkswagen bought the firm in 1991, its UK ads used the self-deprecating 'It's a Škoda, honest' to sell its seriously improved models. Jokes still linger about the older Škodas (the name means damage) in the National Technical Museum. But Škoda is now one of Europe's most successful brands, so it looks like it is having the last laugh.

▶ What do you call a Škoda with twin exhaust pipes? A wheelbarrow.

▶ How do you double the value of a Škoda? Fill the petrol tank.

▶ A guy walks into a garage and asks 'Can you give me a petrol cap for my Škoda?' The mechanic thinks about it briefly and replies, 'OK, sounds like a fair swap.'

▶ What's the difference between a door-to-door salesman and a Škoda? You can shut the door on a door-to-door salesman.

---

### Výstaviště

PERFORMANCE VENUE

13  Map p126, B2

The ornate wrought-iron Výstaviště building, erected for the 1891 Jubilee Exhibition, features the kitsch **Křižíkova Fountain** (www.krizikovafontana .cz; shows 200Kč; ☉performance times vary, usually from 7-10pm Mar-Oct), where frequent short ballets and performances are staged by the Prague Theatre Ballet. (☎220 103 111; Ⓜ Nádraží Holešovice, 🚊5, 12, 14, 15, 17 to Výstaviště)

# Shopping

### Pivní Galerie

BEER

14 🔒 Map p126, E2

A quick tram ride from central Prague and you can purchase beers from across the Czech Republic – we counted around 170 from more than 30 breweries. Note the limited opening hours, and maybe head to Pivovarský Klub (p67) for a slightly smaller range *every* day of the week. (www.pivnigalerie. cz; U průhonu 9; ☉noon-1:30pm & 3-7pm Tue-Fri; 🚊1, 3, 5, 25)

# The Best of
# Prague

Church of Our Lady Before Týn
GLENN VAN DER KNIJFF/LONELY PLANET IMAGES ©

# Best Walks
## Kafka's Prague

### 🏃 The Walk

'This narrow circle encompasses my entire life', Franz Kafka (1883–1924) once said, drawing an outline around Prague's Old Town. While an exaggeration – he travelled and died abroad – Prague is a constant, unspoken presence in Kafka's writing, and this walk through the Old Town passes some of his regular haunts.

**Start** Náměstí Republiky; Ⓜ Náměstí Republiky

**Finish** Hotel Intercontinental; Ⓜ Staroměstská

**Length** 2.6km; 40 minutes

### ✖ Take a Break

Near the Spanish Synagogue in Prague's old Jewish neighbourhood, **Bakeshop Praha** (p65) is a perfect corner spot for gourmet coffee and pastries.

One-time home of Kafka, Old Town Sq

### ❶ Worker's Accident Insurance Company

The author's fiction was influenced by his job as an insurance clerk in an earlier, sometimes brutal, industrial era. Kafka was employed for 14 years (1908–22) at the **Worker's Accident Insurance Company** on Na poříčí. Heading home each day, he'd pass the **Powder Gate** (p77) and **Municipal House** (p77), which was then new.

### ❷ House of the Three Kings

Just before the Old Town Sq on Celetná is the **House of the Three Kings**, where the Kafkas lived from 1896 to 1907. Here Franz first had his own room, overlooking the **Church of Our Lady Before Týn** (p73), and wrote his first story.

### ❸ Sixt House

Across Celetná, the **Sixt House** was an earlier childhood home (1888–89), and just metres away on Staroměstské náměstí is **At the Unicorn**, the home of Berta Fanta's regular literary salon.

## ❹ House of the Minute

The **House of the Minute**, the Renaissance corner building attached to the Old Town Hall, was where Franz lived as a young boy (1889–96), being reluctantly dragged – he later recalled – to his school in Masná street by the family cook.

## ❺ Kafka's Birthplace

Just west of the **Church of St Nicholas** (p73) is **Kafka's birthplace**, marked by a bust of the author at náměstí Franze Kafky 3 (formerly U Radnice 5).

## ❻ Kafka's Bachelor Pad

Despite several fraught love affairs, Kafka never married and mostly lived with his parents. But one of his few **bachelor flats** is found at Dlouhá 16.

## ❼ Bílkova Apartment

Continuing north past the **Franz Kafka monument** (p65) and the **Spanish Synagogue** (p61) you'll come to another of Kafka's temporary **apartments** at Bílkova 22. In 1914 he began *The Trial* here.

## ❽ Hotel Intercontinental

Finally, head west to Pařížská and north towards the river. In the **Hotel Intercontinental's grounds** stood another Kafka family apartment (1907–13), where Franz wrote his Oedipal short story *The Judgment* (1912) and began *Metamorphosis,* about a man transformed into a giant insect.

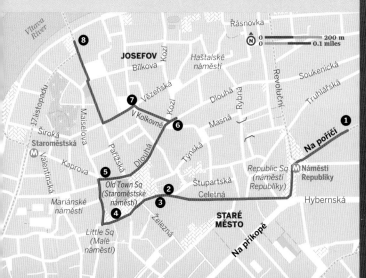

# Best Walks
# Velvet Revolution

## 🏃 The Walk

It's been more than two decades since 1989's Velvet Revolution – when Czechs peacefully overthrew their communist masters – but it will always be a landmark event. This walk takes you past the sites of the large-scale protests, strikes and press conferences that heralded change in the Czech Republic.

**Start** Národní Třída; M Národní Třída

**Finish** Radio Free Europe Building; M Muzeum

**Length** 2.4km; 30 minutes

## ✕ Take a Break

Just off Wenceslas Sq in a faded but formerly glamorous shopping gallery, **Kavárna Lucerna** (p96) is an atmospheric place for coffee or a beer.

Memorial to Jan Palach and Jan Zajíc, Wenceslas Sq

### ❶ Student Memorial

The walk starts where the revolution itself began. Today, there's a **bronze sculpture** under the arches here, marking the Masakr (massacre) of 17 November 1989 – when 50,000 students on an official march to remember Czechs murdered during WWII were attacked by riot police.

### ❷ Adria Palace

Vaclav Havel's Civic Forum set up office at the beautiful **Adria Palace** after the Masakr, holding daily press conferences and threatening a general strike.

### ❸ Wenceslas Statue

The Masakr in Národní třída outraged the nation, and hundreds of thousands of protestors flooded into Wenceslas Sq the next night, staying for weeks. Approach the **Wenceslas Statue** (p91), which itself became a 'revolutionary', bedecked with flags, posters and political slogans.

## ❹ Jan Palach Memorial

The nearby **Jan Palach Memorial** (p91) was the protesters' ad-hoc monument to earlier martyr Jan Palach, who set himself on fire to protest against the Soviet crackdown on 1968's liberal 'Prague Spring'.

## ❺ Činoherní Klub Theatre

Meanwhile, Prague theatres swapped drama for public discussions. Head to **Činoherní Klub Theatre** on Ve Smečkách, where Civic Forum, the key dissident group led by playwright Václav Havel, formed on 19 November. It immediately demanded communist resignations and an investigation into the Masakr.

## ❻ Melantrich Building

On 24 November, as 400,000 demonstrators waited for Havel to address them from the balcony of the **Melantrich building**, the deposed 'Prague Spring' president Alexander Dubček emerged first instead. He was reappearing in public after 20 years of enforced obscurity, and he greeted the crowd: '*Czechoslovensko!*' ('Czechoslovakia!').

## ❼ Radio Free Europe Building

On the third day of the Velvet Revolution, **Radio Free Europe** (see p91) – one media source not controlled by the Communist Party – reported that a student had been killed by police during a protest. The story, though later proven false, prompted even more Czechs to join the demonstrations.

# Best Walks
# **Prague River Walk**

## 🏃 The Walk

Fans of Milan Kundera associate the famed Vltava River with scenes from *The Unbearable Lightness of Being*. Less philosophical types will also enjoy this scenic stroll along (and across) the river – provided you're up for some physical exercise.

**Start** Convent of St Agnes; Ⓜ Staroměstská

**Finish** Dancing Building; Ⓜ Karlovo Náměstí

**Length** 10km; two hours

## 🍴 Take a Break

Perched on the river's edge, old-fashioned **Kavárna Slavia** (p105) is the place to stop for coffee and cake – though not necessarily for a meal. Manoeuvre for a table by the big windows facing Prague Castle.

RICHARD NEBESKÝ/LONELY PLANET IMAGES ©

Vltava River

### ❶ Convent of St Agnes

Start the river walk outside the **Convent of St Agnes**, the oldest Gothic building in Bohemia – building began in 1231. It's named after Princess Agnes, humanitarian and founder of the only Czech religious order in the 13th century. It's supposedly haunted by the ghost of a nun who was killed by her own father after falling in love with a young man.

### ❷ Letná Gardens

Crossing Czech's Bridge, look out over the river and take in the sun-dappled sights of the castle complex and Petřín Hill. Continue to the heights of **Letná Gardens** (p127), stopping for a beer amid jaw-dropping views and a lively local crowd at the hilltop **Letná Beer Garden** (p128).

### ❸ Prague Castle

Continue on to **Prague Castle** (p24). Enjoy the breeze – and sweeping views over the Vltava and the red roofs of Malá Strana – from the ramparts or from a park bench in the beautifully manicured royal gardens built up along the hillside.

## ④ Charles Bridge

Meander downhill towards another of Prague's chief attractions: the bustling and always gorgeous **Charles Bridge** (p74). Midway across the bridge, find a quiet spot to admire your surroundings – the towering medieval gates, the castle, the lazy river, the skyline of Malá Strana, the green slope of Petřín Hill.

## ⑤ Slav Island

To get closer to the water's edge, step onto **Slav Island** (p103). When the weather's warm, you can rent a paddleboat from the stand at one end. Anytime of year, it's a delightfully quiet place to enjoy a picnic or take a nap in the shade.

## ⑥ Dancing Building

Back on the mainland, continue south along the river's edge until you reach the whimsical yet elegant **Dancing**

**Building** (p103). From the outside, it's an obligatory photo op. You can also go upstairs and dine at classy **Céleste** (p103). From this 7th-floor vantage point, you can relax and drink in sunset views of the Vltava over dinner or a glass of wine.

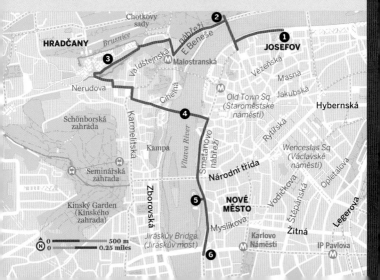

# Best Bars & Pubs

CHRISTER FREDRIKSSON/LONELY PLANET IMAGES ©

In the Czech Republic, drinking is a national pastime. It's no surprise, then, that Prague is an imbiber's playground: on practically every corner, there's another pub, wine bar, beer hall or cocktail lounge. Though it's traditionally been a beer drinker's city, the landscape is changing – a growing interest in national and international wines, plus a trend towards classic cocktails, are diversifying the scene.

## The Beer Basics

When it comes to *pivo* (beer), Pilsner Urquell remains a top Czech brand, but only Budvar remains Czech-owned. However, many pubs produce their own microbrews and these are frequently the best treat. Czech beer, like German, shuns chemicals and uses only water, hops, yeast and barley. In pubs, you'll find it in two main varieties – *světlé* (light) and *tmavy* or *černé* (dark). The *světlé* is a pale amber, modern lager. Dark beers are sweeter and more full-bodied.

## Pub Etiquette

Most draught beer is sold in 0.5L glasses, and you can usually order without saying anything; when the waiter approaches, just raise your thumb for one beer, thumb and index finger for two etc. Even a nod will do. Your bill is recorded on a slip of paper on your table; don't write on it or lose it. As soon as your glass nears empty, another will appear. If you don't want more, place a beer mat over your glass. To pay up and go, say *zaplatím* (I'll pay) or *zaplatíme* (we'll pay). It's normal to tip.

## Best for Beer

**Baráčnická rychta** (p52) A 19th-century beer hall practically hidden on a Malá Strana side street.

**Potrefena Husá Na Verandách** (p57) In Smíchov's original Staropramen Brewery, beer has been brewed since 1871.

**Kolkovna** (p66) At this *tankovna* pub, ice-cold beer flows from polished brass taps.

**U Rudolfina** (p66) One of the only Old Town *pivnices* that doesn't actively woo tourists.

**Pivovarský Klub** (p67) Scores of brews from around the Czech Republic (and the rest of the world).

Beer garden at Riegrovy sady, Vinohrady

**Riegrovy Sady Park Café** (p112) A huge German-style beer garden.

**Letná Beer Garden** (p128) Another beer garden; this one has stunning views over Prague.

**Pivovar u Bulovky** (p128) A range of award-winning beers at this legendary but laid-back pub.

## Best for Cocktails

**Tretter's New York Bar** (p66) A sultry 1930s Manhattan-style cocktail bar.

**Bar & Books** (p81) Classy drinks at this literary-themed watering hole.

**Zanzibar** (p52) Ancient vaulted ceilings and a list of more than 200 cocktails.

**Hapu** (p113) Killer drinks made with freshly squeezed fruit juices.

## Best Wine Bars

**Vinograf** (p52) Choose from 20 wines by the glass to pair with small plates, cheese or olives.

**Bokovka** (p104) Named after the movie *Sideways* (*bokovka* in Czech) and owned by filmmaking wine lovers.

**Kaaba** (p113) This stylish spot boasts an extensive list of Czech and imported wines.

## Best Cafes

**Grand Café Orient** (p81) A stunning cubist gem with a sunny balcony.

**Café Louvre** (p105) Prague's most amenable grand cafe and billiards hall.

**Municipal House Café** (p83) A legendary Viennese-style coffee house inside the art-nouveau landmark.

**Café Savoy** (p49) This gorgeous coffee house does a lavish breakfast.

**Lobkowicz Palace Café** (p37) The elegant new cafe on the ground level of Lobkowicz Palace in Prague Castle.

# Best Food

RICHARD NEBESKY/LONELY PLANET IMAGES ©

Eating out in Prague is a hit-and-miss affair; the restaurant that doesn't regularly have an off night here seems to be a rare thing. Venues your friends, acquaintances and – heaven forbid – your guidebook swear by are never accident-proof. You'll generally have good luck sticking to Czech classics: meat and potatoes washed down with a cold beer.

### Czech Cuisine

The most ubiquitous Czech meal is *vepřová pečeně s knedlíky a kyselé zelí* (roast pork with dumplings and sauerkraut, often abbreviated to *vepřo-knedlo-zelo*). The pork is rubbed with salt and caraway seeds, and roasted long and slow. Other staples include *vepřové kolínko* (pork knuckle), *svíčková na smetaně* (slices of marinated roast beef served with a sour-cream sauce garnished with lemon and cranberries) and *guláš* (a casserole of beef or pork in a tomato, onion and paprika gravy).

Poultry – *kuře* (chicken) and *kachna* (duck) – is popular; *kapr* (carp) is the most traditional Czech fish. At the pub, Czechs have *Smažený sýr* (fried cheese) and *Pražska šunka* (cured and smoked Prague ham).

### International & Vegetarian Options

Despite the locals' predilections, vegetarians can find an ever-increasing number of dining options in Prague today. There's at least one traditional dish you can try – *bramboráky* (potato pancakes). Of course, for *bezmasá jídla* (meat-free dishes) you'll also have great luck at the city's various Italian and Asian eateries.

## ☑ Top Tips

▶ Extras often come at a price – wave away items you didn't order or want, such as baskets of bread, condiments and, in more touristy places, 'free' drinks.

▶ Some places charge for each diner (per cover or *couvert*) and others add a service charge to the bill – and still expect you to tip the usual 10% to 15%.

Kampa Park

### Best Fine Dining

**Kampa Park** (p50) If it's good enough for Mick Jagger and Bill Clinton...

**Bellevue** (p78) Upscale French food and stunning castle views from the terrace.

**U zlaté hrušky** (p37) Visiting dignitaries go to this upscale Czech and international eatery in Nový Svět Quarter.

**Pálffy Palác** (p50) Faded grandeur, palace gardens and French food.

**Céleste** (p103) French food on the 7th floor of the famed Dancing Building.

### Best Czech Cuisine

**V Zátiší** (p79) Sophisticated tasting menus give Czech food an elegant twist.

**U Ferdinanda** (p95) A modern spin on a classic Czech pub with a funky garden and great goulash.

**Restaurace U Šumavy** (p104) Proof that good-value Bohemian food still exists in central Prague.

### Best for Vegetarians

**Lehká Hlava** (p79) Creative international menu and glowing marble tables.

**Beas Vegetarian Dhaba** (p80) This friendly Indian restaurant does self-service vegetarian curries.

**Klub Architektů** (p80) The architects' society offers plenty of meat-free dishes.

**Malý Buddha** (p38) Thai dishes and 'healing wines' near Prague Castle.

### Best for a Quick Lunch

**Ristorante Pasta Fresca** (p80) Italian gourmet pizza and pasta near Old Town Sq.

**Bakeshop Praha** (p65) A stylish bakery in the Jewish Quarter.

**Noodles** (p95) Retro design and noodles from around the world.

# Best
# Art

For a general overview, a first-time visitor to Prague could break down the city's art scene into three camps: royal art (anything to do with Prague Castle and its collections), Czech cubism (the locals were actually the first to apply cubist principles to architecture and furniture) and avant-garde modern art (David Černý's cutting-edge modern art is everywhere, both in public settings and private museums).

RICHARD NEBESKY/LONELY PLANET IMAGES ©

## Best Art Museums

**Museum of Czech Cubism** (p78) A proud reminder that the Czechs were pioneers in the application of cubist principles to architecture and furniture.

**Mucha Museum** (p93) See the Czech maestro's pretty maidens on fin-de-siècle Parisian advertisements.

**Veletržní Palace** (p124) Houses the National Gallery's jaw-dropping collection of 20th- and 21st-century Czech and European art.

**Prague Castle Picture Gallery** (p29) With works by Rubens, Tintoretto and Titian.

**Schwarzenberg Palace** (p35) Renaissance and baroque masterpieces.

**Kampa Museum** (p47) This flour-mill-turned-gallery houses Central European artworks.

**Futura Centre for Contemporary Art** (p57) Smíchov's pride and joy is home to David Černý's edgy, oversized *Brownnosing*.

**DOX Centre for Contemporary Art** (p127) Prague's most capacious gallery space hosts thought-provoking contemporary art and photography.

## Best Public Art

**Hanging Out sculpture** (p78) Another of David Černý's whimsical, slightly off-the-wall public artworks.

**Mucha's painted-glass windows** (p31) Inside Prague Castle's St Vitus Cathedral.

**Piss** (p45) David Černý's sculpture *Proudy* (pictured above) features two guys relieving themselves into a puddle shaped like the Czech Republic.

**Franz Kafka Monument** (p65) This unusual sculpture has a mini-Franz sitting piggyback on his own headless body.

**Cubist Lamppost** (p93) The world's one and only.

# Best
# **Museums**

Prague's not exactly a big museum city – perhaps because with its fascinating castle, royal grounds, architecture and ancient bridges, the city itself is like one huge outdoor museum – and the admission is free. Prague Castle, too, is essentially an extensive museum. These smaller attractions are best for special-interest travellers and rainy days.

There's one major exception to the rule – Prague is home to several good art museums (listed under Best Art) and the fantastic Jewish Museum, which actually comprises six distinct synagogues and monuments in the former Jewish ghetto of Josefov. If you don't see any other museums in Prague, at least make a point to get to the Jewish Museum and the adjacent Jewish Cemetery.

**Franz Kafka Museum**
(p47) The writer's original documents and photos.

**Jewish Museum** (p60) Comprises six important Jewish sites; this museum was the city's most visited in 2010.

**Miniatures Museum** (p36) A delightfully quirky collection of miniature artworks.

**Charles Bridge Museum** (p75) When you learn about the bridge's tumultuous 650-year history, you'll be surprised it's still standing.

**National Museum** (p95) The huge museum is undergoing renovations; see exhibits at the New Building instead.

DOUG MCKINLAY/LONELY PLANET IMAGES ©

## ☑ **Top Tips**

▶ Check online for current promotions: many museums offer free admission on a certain day each month, or discounted admission for certain travellers.

▶ For the best art museums, see the 'Best Art' list.

▶ Remember that photography is highly restricted in many of the city's museums and attractions – ask before snapping.

# Best
# **History**

RICHARD NEBESKY/LONELY PLANET IMAGES ©

It's impossible to quickly summarise Prague's long and colourful past. The city's most noteworthy historical sites often relate to one of the most important events and/or time periods – the royal heyday in and around Prague Castle, the Hussite Wars, WWI and WWII, the rise and fall of communism and the Velvet Revolution.

### Religious Versus Royal

The city's religious history – best told on a walking tour of its various ancient churches and historic synagogues – intertwines with Prague's royal past, best understood by spending half a day at Prague Castle, the most notable historic district. Founded by Czech 'Přemysl' princes in the 9th century, Pražský hrad is still the official presidential residence. The world's largest castle complex, bigger than seven football fields, it dominates this city of 1.2 million.

Though much of the castle consists of imperial residences and palaces, the grounds also house several of Prague's most important religious centres, including the Gothic-style St Vitus Cathedral and the Romanesque St George's Basilica. Slightly further afield, in surrounding Hradčany, important royal residences like Černín Palace and religious sites like the Loreta – a noted place of pilgrimage – line the cobblestone streets in nearly equal measure.

### Quirky Prague

Another story, sometimes more intriguing, unfolds as you visit Prague's lesser-known historic sites: the high window a man 'fell' through to his own death, a beautiful decorative object made with thousands of diamonds once owned by a filthy-rich countess, the mural that young Czech liberals repainted over and over again even as secret police tried to destroy it.

### Best Quirky History Sites

**Černín Palace** (p36) Site of Jan Masaryk's defenestration.

**Tomb of St John of Nepomuk** (p31) Nepomuk was canonised after his tongue was found allegedly 'still alive' centuries after his death.

**Prague Sun** (p33) Donated by a rich (and generous) countess, this artwork is studded with 6222 diamonds.

**Petřín Lookout Tower** (p43) The mini Eiffel tower was built in 1891 for the Prague Exposition.

**Lennon Wall** (p48) This graffiti-splattered memorial was repainted each time the secret police whitewashed over it.

Library of the Strahov Monastery

## Best Landmarks

**Astronomical Clock**
(p73) The ancient mechanical marvel that still chimes on the hour.

**Jan Hus Monument**
(p77) Honours the Czech hero burned at the stake for heresy in 1415.

**Powder Gate** (p77) This 15th-century structure towers dramatically over Old Town.

**Wenceslas Square**
(p90) Site of public executions and Velvet Revolution protests.

## Best for Special Interests

**Clementinum** (p78)
The National Library is located inside this monastery-turned–Jesuit university.

**Jewish Cemetery** (p62)
The 'garden of the dead' in the old Jewish ghetto has more than 12,000 tombstones.

**Orthodox Cathedral of SS Cyril & Methodius** (p103) The site where seven Czech partisans took refuge from the Nazis – and met tragic ends – in 1942.

## Best Churches & Synagogues

**St Vitus Cathedral**
(p30) The largest and most important church in the Czech Republic.

**Old-New Synagogue**
(p65) Europe's oldest working synagogue.

**Strahov Monastery**
(p35) Contains the fabulously grand Strahov Library.

**Church of Our Lady Victorious** (p47) Housing the famous 'Infant of Prague'.

**Spanish Synagogue**
(p61) Prague's most beautiful synagogue has an ornate Moorish interior.

**Church of St Nicholas**
(detail pictured above left; p47) Prague's finest baroque building.

# Best
# For Kids

DOUG MCKINLAY/LONELY PLANET IMAGES ©

Like a city straight out of a picture book, Prague is a charming destination for children. Little ones will be enchanted by Prague Castle; they'll also get a kick out of the Miniatures Museum, have fun riding the tram and poking around traditional Czech toy shops; and they'll love riding the funicular train up Petřín Hill, and letting loose in the city's green parks and gardens.

## Best of the Outdoors

**Petřín Funicular** (p43) Kids will get a thrill riding this funicular up to the top of the hill, then hiking back down.

**Slav Island** (p103) Rent a paddleboat and enjoy a ride on the Vltava.

**Stromovka** (p128) Prague's largest central park; kids like climbing on the ancient branches of an ancient fallen tree.

**Letná Gardens** (p127) Outdoor fun and views; for the parents, there's a beer garden, too.

**Riegrovy sady** (p117) Another lovely green space with a beer garden serving food and drink.

**Vyšehrad** (p108) When city chaos is too much, retreat with the kids to this breezy green space.

## Best Indoor Activities

**Pohádka** (p87) Shop for high-quality, traditional Czech toys here.

**Bio Oko** (p128) This art-house cinema features frequent children's events.

**Miniatures Museum** (p36) Tiny exhibits and curiosities spark kids' imaginations at this delightful little museum.

**Rocking Horse Toy Shop** (p39) A charming toy shop near the castle.

**Laterna Magika** (p107) Kids love the optical illusions onstage during the 'Black Light' theatre performances here.

 **Top Tips**

▶ Kids' admission is discounted to almost every attraction in the city; inquire about age cut-offs and be sure to bring teenagers' and college students' ID cards to prove their status.

# Best
# For Free

TIM HUGHES / LONELY PLANET IMAGES ©

You can take in many of Prague's delights – the architecture, the famous bridges, the parks and gardens, views of the castle – without spending anything. In fact, the city is so walkable that you don't even need to budget for transport. Just wear comfortable shoes and hit the cobble-stoned streets with an open mind.

**Prague Castle** (p24) Wander through these spectacular royal grounds, including the stunning gardens, without spending a crown.

**St Vitus Cathedral** (p30) It's free to walk into the famous cathedral, though you'll have to pay to enter certain areas.

**Nový Svět Quarter** (p35) A delightful alternative to Prague Castle's Golden Lane.

**Petřín Hill** (p42) Entrance to the famous park is gratis; skip the funicular and just hike up.

**Astronomical Clock** (p73) The hourly chiming is public and free.

**Charles Bridge** (p74) A stroll across the ancient bridge is essential and, of course, sans admission fee.

**Slav Island** (p103) As long as you don't feel the urge to rent a paddleboat, Slav Island's peace and quiet doesn't cost anything.

**Vyšehrad Cemetery** (p109) Check out Mucha's final resting place for free.

**Stromovka** (p128) Run and play to your heart's content in this sprawling outdoor playground.

**Letná Gardens** (p127) The sweeping views are free; beers from the beer garden cost extra.

## ☑ Top Tips

▸ Some museums offer free admission on certain days of the month; check reviews for details.

▸ Ask at tourist information offices about free concerts, theatrical performances and cultural events happening during your visit.

▸ Though entrance to the Prague Castle complex is free, you'll have to pay for entrance into many sites.

# Best
# **Architecture**

JONATHAN SMITH/LPI © ARCHITECT FRANK GEHRY

Prague is often called an 'open-air museum of architecture', and it's no exaggeration. Not only have the neighbourhoods of Hradčany, Malá Strana, Staré Město and Nové Město jointly been granted Unesco World Heritage listing, nearly half of the city's 3500 buildings are designated cultural monuments.

### Royal Style & the Gothic Look

The earliest architecture is Romanesque from the later Přemysl princes of the 10th to 12th centuries. These Czech nobles, responsible for Prague Castle, commissioned buildings with heavy stone walls and small windows. The Gothic style, typified by tall, pointed arches, spindly spires and ribbed vaults, is associated with a proud era in Czech history. This is when Charles IV made Prague the capital of the Holy Roman Empire and began commissioning monuments such as St Vitus Cathedral and Charles Bridge.

### National Revival & Art Nouveau

In the early 16th century the Habsburgs invited Italian designers and architects to create the Habsburg idea of a royal city. The Italians brought an enthusiasm for classical form, grace, symmetry and exuberant decoration. After the Great Fire of 1541, Hradčany and Malá Strana were rebuilt in this style.

During the so-called Czech National Revival, major new public buildings were commissioned, including the National Theatre and the National Museum. Architects then began to express their national aspirations through art nouveau (c 1899–1912); the Municipal House is a beautiful example.

## ☑ **Top Tips**

▶ For more on Prague architecture, take a specialised tour such as Thousand Years of Prague Architecture (www. walkingtours.cz).

▶ Check out 'What is Czech Cubism?', the Modernista website and online gallery (www.mod ernista.cz).

▶ *Prague: An Architectural Guide* is a photographic encyclopaedia by Mark Smith, Michal Schonberh and Radomira Sedlakova.

Church of St Nicholas (p73) at Old Town Sq

## Best Renaissance & Baroque Architecture

**St George's Basilica** (p29) The interior is a fine example of the early Romanesque style.

**Schwarzenberg Palace** (p35) The facade is an example of *sgraffito*, a multilayered mural technique creating a 3D effect.

**Church of St Nicholas** (p73) The striking dome is a symbol of Old Town Prague.

**Loreta** (p32) The pilgrimage site is modelled after the Italian original.

## Best Gothic & Neo-Gothic Architecture

**St Vitus Cathedral** (p30) Gothic to the tips of its famous spires.

**Charles Bridge** (p74) Prague's most famous bridge is a Gothic landmark.

**Powder Gate** (p77) The neo-Gothic tower once served as storage space for gunpowder.

## Best Art-Nouveau Architecture

**Municipal House** (p77) Glittering art nouveau in top form.

**Kavárna Evropa** (p91) Fading grandeur at this ornate art-nouveau hotel and cafe.

**Výstaviště** (p131) Home to the whimsical 'Dancing Fountain'.

## Best Modern Work

**Dancing Building** (pictured above left; p103) The shape of the building mimics a dancing couple.

**Veletržní Palace** (p124) This mammoth functionalist structure doesn't look like your everyday palace.

# Best
# Shopping

RICHARD NEBESKY/LONELY PLANET IMAGES ©

Although its streets are lined with stores, Prague doesn't initially seem a particularly inspiring shopping destination. But if you know where to look, you can find above-average versions of the classic Czech souvenirs: Bohemian crystal and glassware, garnet and amber jewellery, wooden marionettes, and shoes. Think outside the box: Czech liquor, farm-produced beauty products and classic children's toys all make great gifts.

For a spot of mainstream shopping, Na příkopě boasts international chains from H&M to Zara and some of the city's most famous malls. For the most part, you can put your wallet away along Wenceslas Sq (not a bad idea anyway, considering the pickpocketing that goes on here). Instead, explore the Old Town's winding alleyways. Ritzy Pařížská is often called Prague's Champs Elysées and, although it's far smaller, it is lined with luxury brands like Cartier, Dolce & Gabbana, Hugo Boss and Ferragamo. Dlouhá, Dušní and surrounding streets house some original fashion boutiques, while even central Celetná contains a worthwhile stop or two.

## Best for Unique Souvenirs

**Botanicus** (p85) Rustic-chic beauty products from this popular old apothecary.

**Kotva** (p69) Well-priced Bohemian glass in this local department store.

**Manufaktura** (p86) Specialises in Czech traditional crafts and wooden toys.

**Art Deco Galerie** (p87) Czech antiques galore; hunt for treasures here on a rainy day.

**Bat'a** (p98) The 1929 flagship store of the great Czech footwear line.

## Best for Design Geeks

**Modernista** (p86) Showcasing Czech cubist and art-deco design with cool ceramics, jewellery, posters and books.

**Qubus** (p69) Quirky homewares by Czech designers.

**Moser** (p98) Ornate Bohemian glass objects.

## Best Accessories

**Granát Turnov** (p69) The largest national manufacturer of garnet jewellery.

**Kebab** (p69) The coolest streetwear boutique in Prague.

# Best
# **Nightlife**

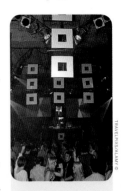

TRAVELPIX/ALAMY ©

No one comes to Prague specifically for serious or cutting-edge clubbing, particularly when hipper Berlin is so near. There's plenty of nightlife here, and big-name bands and DJs put in the occasional appearance, but this is not a place for chasing the latest European trends. Instead, it's a destination for letting down your hair and revelling in some unpretentious fun.

Musically, dance clubs have a penchant for 1980s and '90s pop; locals reckon the predilection for '80s tunes in particular is a rose-tinted, if slightly ironic, nostalgia for the simpler, more controlled days of communism. Prague also has many basement music clubs, DJ bars and edgy 'experimental' venues. Roxy and Žižkov's Palác Akropolis present the best of up-and-coming overseas acts. If you're serious about clubbing, do as the locals do and head to Holešovice where the city's authentic nightlife spots just happen to be clustered.

## Best Upscale Nightclubs

**M1 Lounge** (p66) The central dance club has plush seating, *shishas* and sushi until 3am.

**Infinity** (p119) This mid-sized cellar alternates between upbeat happy house and nostalgic '60s to '90s nights.

**Mecca** (p128) A slice of Ibiza in the Prague suburbs.

**SaSaZu** (p129) A 'super-club' where international DJs play in a UFO-styled booth.

## Best for Live Music

**Roxy** (p69) DJs and live bands rock inside the dilapidated shell of an art-deco cinema.

**Palác Akropolis** (p121) A sticky-floored shrine to alternative music and drama.

## ☑ **Top Tips**

▶ Go late. The dance floors are rarely ever populated before midnight.

▶ There's no dress code – wear what you want.

▶ Check the clubs' listings ahead of time to find out about DJ line-ups and themed nights.

# Best
## Culture

DOUG MCKINLAY/LONELY PLANET IMAGES ©

As the city where Mozart chose to premiere *Don Giovanni*, and the birthplace of vaunted composers like Antonín Dvořák, Leoš Janáček and Bedřich Smetana, Prague has a long, proud tradition of opera and classical music. Add to that some beautiful theatres and very cheap tickets, and it's no mystery as to why the city has become a much-touted opera destination.

### Opera & Classical Music

Of the three venues where opera is performed – the National Theatre, the Estates Theatre and the State Opera – the first is the most highly rated. Attending a classical concert is also a good bet, especially if you book tickets for the Czech Philharmonic Orchestra at the Rudolfinum. During festivals such as the Prague Spring, international orchestras also appear in the city.

### Jazz

Prague is the city in which former US president Bill Clinton revealed his skill with a saxophone in the 1990s. Czechs figured prominently in European jazz circles from the 1920s until the 1948 communist coup d'état, and even under communism the art form survived. Prague' s first professional jazz club, Reduta, opened during the less censorial atmosphere of the 1960s. There's still a jazz sensibility at large in the city today.

### Pop & Rock

The folky 'Czech Pogues' Čechomor have toured internationally, and the spacey Sunflower Caravan and the Smiths–influenced Southpaw are both worth catching.

☑ **Top Tips**

▶ Choose your own seats at the big theatres – for a small fee – through their websites.

▶ Websites like www.praguepost. com, www.prague. tv and www.expats. cz have information on upcoming gigs by international acts. Buy tickets online and check upcoming shows at www. ticketpro.cz.

National Theatre

## Best Classical Theatres

**State Opera House** (p97) Gorgeous ballet and opera performances are staged in this beautiful neo-rococo theatre.

**National Theatre** (p106) Has an excellent reputation for drama, opera and ballet.

**Estates Theatre** (p85) Mozart premiered and conducted *Don Giovanni* here in 1787.

**Smetana Hall** (p85) Home of the Prague Symphony Orchestra.

**Rudolfinum** (p67) Dvořák Hall is home to the Czech Philharmonic.

## Best Jazz

**AghaRTA Jazz Centrum** (p85) A classic jazz cellar hosting occasional international acts.

**U Malého Glena** (p54) Intimate venue for consistently good jazz.

**Reduta Jazz Club** (p107) Bill Clinton played the sax at Prague's oldest jazz club.

## Best Alternative Venues

**MeetFactory** (p57) David Černý's gallery, exhibition space and entertainment venue in Smíchov.

**Kino Světozor** (p97) The only central Prague cinema for European art-house movies and cult documentaries.

**Laterna Magika** (p107) Stages 'Black Light' theatre.

# Best
# Gay & Lesbian

DOUG MCKINLAY/LONELY PLANET IMAGES ©

Prague has a medium-sized gay and lesbian scene. In the past few years a definite 'gay quarter' (or 'gaybourhood') has developed, just out of central Prague in Vinohrady. With top venues Club ON, Termix and Saints leading the way, there are now at least 10 venues all within 10 minutes of each other, in and around the metro station of Náměstí Míru.

According to one regular, the scene is very easy-going. There's no 'face control', or dress code at the door, and even the top venues don't charge entrance fees. To all intents and purposes, homophobia barely exists in Prague. (Czechs are too laid-back to be prejudiced, one resident suggests!) There are also no problems with rampaging British stag parties, which are fewer in number these days, but who stick to the centre in any case. Generally, gay and lesbian couples will feel more than comfortable in any of the nightlife spots we recommend in this book.

## Best Gay Bars & Clubs

**Termix** (p120) An industrial-style bar with a small but happening dance floor.

**Club ON** (p120) Formerly Valentino, it's the city's gay superclub.

**Saints** (p119) This British-run gay bar is laid-back and friendly.

☑ **Top Tips**

▶ Dress neatly but casually – as elsewhere in Prague, the dress code is laid-back.

▶ Although things differ bar to bar, the scene is very mixed between Czechs and foreigners.

▶ For English speakers, an excellent first stop is Saints, which runs a gay travel and accommodation service and maintains an up-to-date website with an interactive map of the scene.

# Survival Guide

# Survival Guide

# Before You Go

## When to Go

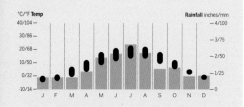

°C/°F Temp
Rainfall inches/mm

40/104 — — 4/100
30/86 — — 3/75
20/68 — — 2/50
10/50 — — 1/25
0/32 — — 0
-10/14 —

J F M A M J J A S O N D

➡ **Winter (Nov–Mar)**
Short, dark days, romantic snow and occasionally blustery winds. Tourist crowds descend on the city for lively Christmas festivities.

➡ **Spring (Apr–Jun)**
Many European tourists visit when the city's parks and gardens are blooming.

➡ **Summer (Jul–Aug)**
All attractions see the most activity during these sunny but usually mild months.

➡ **Autumn (Sep–Oct)**
The weather turns crisp and the trees on Petřín Hill start changing colour– with kids back to school, visitors have more breathing space at the major attractions.

## Book Your Stay

➡ Prague annually accommodates millions of tourists, so it's hardly surprising there is a wealth of places to sleep – but it doesn't always mean great bargains for visitors.

➡ The market is quite polarised, with fantastic five-star establishments, loads of cheap and cheerful hostels, and a relative gap in the midrange market.

➡ You can often find a last-minute bargain for the top-end hotels on all the standard online booking sites.

➡ Most visitors want to stay right in the centre of the city, but be aware that although Wenceslas Sq contains hotels in nearly every price range, the area gets seedy after dark.

➡ Malá Strana is a particularly scenic location in which to stay, but it's worth considering a location in Prague's inner suburbs like Vinohrady, Smíchov and Holešovice, as central Prague is easily reached by public transport.

➡ If you are booking somewhere central, check your room is not facing a busy street, particularly in the Old Town.

## Useful Websites

**Hotels Prague** (www.hotelsprague.cz) Listings of the city's best historic hotels and B&Bs.

**Guide Prague** (www.guideprague.com) Well-run booking site offers plenty of photos.

**AAAAHotels** (www.aaaahotels.com) Efficient apartment and hotel reservations via this customer-service-oriented agency.

**Booking.com** (www.booking.com) Helps you make reservations at hundreds of Prague hotels.

## Best Budget

**Sir Toby's Hostel** (www.sirtobys.com) Traveller favourite in nightlife hub Holešovice.

**Czech Inn** (www.czech-inn.com) This 'design hostel' has a happening cafe.

**Hostel Lipa** (www.hostellipa.com) Stay off the beaten path in cool Žižkov.

**Arcadia Old Town** (www.arcadiaoldtown.com) Budget-friendly apartments in a great Old Town location.

## Best Midrange

**Hotel Neruda** (www.hotelneruda.cz) Lovely restoration of a 14th-century convent.

**Hotel Josef** (www.hoteljosef.com) All-white chic near the Jewish Quarter.

**Hotel at the Three Storks** (www.atthethreestorks.praguehotels.it) A stylish 20-room hotel in a restored old brewery.

**Vintage Design Hotel Sax** (www.hotelsax.cz) Featuring eye-popping colours and lively design.

## Best Top End

**U Zlate Studne** (www.goldenwell.cz) Romantic 17-room boutique hotel beneath Prague Castle.

**Mandarin Oriental** (www.mandarinoriental.com) Luxe digs in quaint Malá Strana.

**Augustine** (www.theaugustine.com) A Rocco Forte hotel in a stunning restored monastery.

**Boscolo Carlo IV** (www.prague.boscolohotels.com) Retro Italian style in this 152-room favourite.

## Best Short-Stay Apartments

**Alchymist Residence Nosticova** (www.nosticova.com) Ten gorgeous apartments in a 17th-century building.

**Emma Apartments** (www.apartments-emma.com) Affordable apartments in Vyšehrad.

**Zderaz Apartments** (www.zderaz.com) Friendly accommodation; the original building dates from the 9th century.

**Charles Bridge Apartments** (www.charlesbridgebb.com) Just steps from the Charles Bridge.

# Arriving in Prague

☑ **Top Tip** For the best way to get to your accommodation, see p17.

## Prague-Ruzyně Airport

This international **airport** (☎220 113 314; www.prg.aero) is 17km west of the city centre.

➡ **Cedaz Shuttlebus**
(www.cedaz.cz) Mini shuttlebuses take travellers to and from the airport to its station on Náměstí Republiky. Daily shuttles leave from both locations every 30 minutes between 7.30am and 7pm; one-way tickets cost 120Kč.

➡ **Airport Express Bus**
Runs between the airport and Prague's main train station, Praha hlavní nádraží, at 30-minute intervals. From the airport, service starts at 5.46am and the last bus leaves at 9.16pm. Purchase a ticket from the driver for 50Kč (25Kč for children aged six to 15 years).

➡ **AAA Taxi** (www.aaa taxi.cz) Prague's most reliable taxi service. To book a taxi inside the airport, look for the AAA desk in the arrivals hall. A ride to Náměstí Republiky will cost about 500Kč (more if you get stuck in traffic.) Beware of hailing other taxis at the airport; if they're not AAA you might get ripped off.

➡ **Bus 119.** Catch the city bus from the airport to the closest metro station, Dejvická, on one end of Line A. Standard

transport fares apply; the current fare for a 90-minute window of time is adult/concession 32/16Kč. If you're toting sizeable luggage, you'll need to pay an extra 16Kč to bring it on the bus.

## Praha hlavní ńdraží

Most international trains arrive at Prague's recently revitalised main station, **Praha hlavní nádraží** (www.dp.cz).

➡ To Old Town, walk or take metro Line A to Staroměstská station.

➡ To get to Prague Castle, take metro Line A to Hradčanská station or Malostranská station.

➡ To get to Wenceslas Sq, just walk (it's two blocks away).

➡ To arrive in Žižkov or Vinohrady, take metro Line A to Jiřiho z Podebrad station.

Note that some trains arrive at Prague's other large train station, Praha-Holešovice, conveniently connected to the Nádraži Holešovice station on the metro's Line C.

## Florenc Bus Station

Not many short-break travellers arrive in Prague by bus, but it's certainly possible at popular travel times when trains are booked – or if you're making a connection from a low-cost flight to surrounding airports like Bratislava.
**Florenc bus station**
(www.jizdniradry.cz; Křžíkova 4, Karlín) is positioned at the junction of the metro's B and C lines. From Florenc, take Line B to Náměstí Republiky to access the Jewish Museum, or to Můstek for Wenceslas Sq and Old Town. At Můstek, travellers can change to Line A to continue onto Prague Castle (Hradčanská or Malostranská stations.) Line C goes to Vyšehrad.

# Getting Around

Prague has an excellent integrated public transport system (www.dpp .cz) of metro, trams, buses and night trams, but when you're moving around the compact old town or the castle area, you might find it more convenient and scenic to use your feet. If you're using the metro system, bank on about one or two minutes per metro stop. Times between tram stops are posted at each stop and on www.dpp.cz.

## Metro

☑ **Best for**... Quick transportation between major sights, connecting to the train station and venturing outside the tourist areas.

➡ The metro operates from 5am to midnight.

➡ There are three lines: Line A (green) runs from Dejvická in the northwest to Depo Hostivař in the east; Line B (yellow) runs from Zličín in the southwest to Černý most in the northeast; and Line C (red) runs from Háje in the southeast to Letňany in the north.

➡ Line A intersects Line C at Muzeum, Line B intersects Line C at Florenc and Line A intersects Line B at Můstek.

➡ Services are fast and frequent. You'll find a map in every metro station and metro train, as well as on the pull-out

map at the back of this book. In this book, the nearest metro station is noted after the Ⓜ in each listing.

➡ A basic 90-minute ride costs adult/concession 32/16Kč, short-term or

30-minute rides go for 24/12Kč. See the Tickets & Passes boxed text for more on daily and three-day passes.

➡ You must buy your ticket (jízdenka) before boarding, and then

## Tickets & Passes

Prague has one of Europe's best public transport systems – it's inexpensive and wonderfully efficient. That said, buying (and using) transport tickets in Prague isn't exactly the most straightforward process. Though the metro, trams and buses all use the same kind of ticket, you can only buy these tickets in metro stations or nearby kiosks – never from the driver, for example. On top of that, it's the traveller's responsibility to properly validate one's ticket. If you're caught riding without a ticket or pass that's been clearly stamped, you'll have to pay a fine – and deal with the trauma of being pulled off the metro by a transport officer who likely doesn't speak two words of English. For most travellers, it's best to avoid the hassle of validating individual tickets, opting instead for a day or three-day pass. Read on for options.

➡**Basic ticket** Valid for 90 minutes; adult/concession 32/16Kč.

➡**Short-term ticket** Valid for 30 minutes; adult/concession 24/12Kč.

➡**One-day ticket** Valid for 24 hours; adult/concession 110/55Kč.

➡**Three-day ticket** Valid for 72 hours; 310Kč for all ages.

➡**Luggage ticket** Necessary for most travellers; 16Kč.

validate it by punching it in the little yellow machine in the metro station lobby or on the bus or tram when you begin your journey. Checks by inspectors are frequent; they'll fine you travelling without a time-stamped ticket (reduced if you pay on the spot). There's also a small fine for not having a luggage ticket (which costs 16Kč above the regular fare.)

➡ You'll need coins for ticket machines at metro stations and major tram stops, but you can pay for tickets with notes at newsstands, *Trafiky* snack shops, PNS newspaper kiosks, hotels, PIS tourist information offices and most metro station ticket offices.

➡ Kids under six travel free.

## Tram & Bus

☑ **Best for**... Scenic rides, connecting to attractions far off the metro lines, and for travellers who can't easily walk from point A to B. Most visitors won't have any reason to get on a bus, but a tram ride is a classic Prague experience.

➡ Important tram lines to remember are 22 (this runs to Prague Castle,

Malá Strana and Charles Bridge), 17 and 18 (these run to the Jewish Quarter and Old Town Sq) and 11 (this runs to Žižkov and Vinohrady).

➡ Regular tram and bus services (see www .dpp.cz for maps and timetables) run from 5am to midnight. After this, night trams (51 to 58) and buses (501 to 512) still rumble across the city about every 40 minutes.

➡ Night trams intersect at Lazarská in Nové Město. If you're planning a late evening, find out if one of these services passes near where you're staying.

➡ Be aware that few tram or bus stops sell tickets. So if you're using single tickets, buy several in the metro station, then save a couple unstamped in your bag or pocket and validate them upon boarding.

➡ As with metro tickets, the fares are as follows: 90-minute ride adult/ concession 32/16Kč, short-term or 30-minute rides 24/12Kč. See the Tickets & Passes boxed text (p161) for more on daily and three-day passes.

## Taxi

☑ **Best for**... Late-night rides back to the hotel, airport transfers, and when you're running late for a show at the National Theatre.

➡ For years, Prague's taxi drivers were renowned for scams and dishonesty. However, huge fines and crackdowns have made a big difference. Most drivers now turn on their meters when picking up a fare, as legally required. If a driver won't comply, find another taxi.

➡ Look for the 'Taxi Fair Place' scheme, which provides authorised taxis in key tourist areas. Drivers can charge a maximum fare and must announce the estimated price in advance.

➡ Away from official 'Taxi Fair Place' stands, the streets around Wenceslas Sq, Národní třída, Na příkopě, Praha hlavní nádraží, Old Town Sq and Malostranské náměstí are the most notorious rip-off spots. Make sure you know the current exchange rate if the driver offers you the chance to pay in a foreign currency.

➡ Within the city centre, trips should be around 150Kč to 200Kč, a trip to the suburbs no more than 450Kč, and to the airport around 600Kč to 700Kč.

In our experience, the following radio-taxi services are all reliable and honest:

**AAA Radio Taxi** (☎14 014, 222 333 222; www.aaataxi.cz)

**Halo Taxi** (☎244 114 411)

**ProfiTaxi** (☎844 700 800)

## Bicycle

☑ **Best for**... Sightseeing and green travellers.

Despite the cobblestones, hills and gigantic tourist buses trying to navigate backstreets, in recent years Prague has become more bike-friendly. Try these outfitters (they're usually closed in winter):

**Praha Bike** (☎732 388 880; www.prahabike.cz; Dlouha 24; ⏱9am-8pm Apr-Oct) Rentals and guided tours in Old Town. Has tandem bikes and will deliver your rental for an extra fee.

**City Bike Prague** (☎776 180 284; www.citybike -prague.com; Královodská 5; ⏱9am-7pm Apr-Oct) Also in Old Town, City Bike has a great selection of wheels. Get a discount by booking online.

# Essential Information

## Business Hours

☑ **Top Tip** Avid shoppers should note that local stores (those not specifically geared to tourists) often close at lunchtime on Saturday and many stay closed on Sunday.

Reviews in this guidebook don't list business hours unless they differ from the following standards:

**Banks** 8am to 4.30pm Monday to Friday

**Bars** 11am to midnight

**Main post office** (Jindřišská 14, Nové Město) 2am to midnight

**Shops** 8.30am to 8pm Monday to Friday, to 6pm Saturday and Sunday

**Restaurants** 10am to 11pm

## Emergency

**EU-wide emergency hotline** (☎112)

**Fire** (☎150)

**Municipal Police** (☎156)

**State Police** (☎158)

## Electricity

230V/50Hz

## Money

☑ **Top Tip** Many private exchange booths in central Prague lure tourists with attractive-looking exchange rates, which they don't actually offer when buying crowns. These are the selling rates or only available when changing huge sums. Check the small print before parting with any money. Better yet, just take money out of your own bank account using the widespread ATMs (*bankomaty*). Credit cards are also widely accepted.

➡ The Czech crown (Koruna česká, or Kč) is divided into 100 hellers (*haléřů*, or h).

➡ Keep small change handy for use in public toilets and tram-ticket machines, and always try to keep some small-denomination notes for shops, cafes and bars.

## Public Holidays

Banks, offices, department stores and some shops will be closed on public holidays. Restaurants, museums and tourist attractions tend to stay open.

**New Year's Day** 1 January

**Easter Monday** March/April

**Labour Day** 1 May

**Liberation Day** 8 May

**SS Cyril & Methodius Day** 5 July

**Jan Hus Day** 6 July

**Czech Statehood Day** 28 September

**Republic Day** 28 October

**Struggle for Freedom & Democracy Day** 17 November

**Christmas Eve** (Generous Day) 24 December

**Christmas Day** 25 December

**St Stephen's Day** 26 December

## Safe Travel

Pickpocketing is unfortunately rife, especially in high season around the main tourist attractions. Keep your valuables well out of reach, and be alert in crowds and on public transport.

The former 'Foreigners Police Station' system was abolished in 2006. Today if you're the victim of theft, simply find the nearest police station and ask to fill out a standard form for insurance purposes. In theory someone should speak English at the **Praha 1 police station** (Jungmannovo náměstí 9; Ⓜ Mustek), but be aware the police don't exactly have a reputation for helpfulness. For passports, contact your embassy (see www.expats.cz for listings).

## Telephone

☑ **Top Tip** If you need to make many local calls – or if you want to have a number where you ca be reliably reached by family and friends back home – buying a Czech SIM card and popping

## Money-Saving Tips

➡ Forget taxis – take a shuttle bus from the airport to the city, then use public transport.

➡ Skip the sushi and eat Czech food; you'll find the best value for your crowns in the locals' favourite restaurants. Look for set-lunch specials.

➡ Remember that many local dishes are large enough to share. A Czech beer is twice the size of a beer you might order in a pub at home.

➡ Don't exchange cash at the airport. Extract the local currency with your ATM card instead.

➡ When going to the theatre, book the cheapest seats (usually around 100Kč.) In a venue as gorgeous as the State Opera House or the National Theatre; even the nosebleed seats are wonderful.

➡ Don't worry about missing museums if your budget is an issue – this is a city best explored outdoors and on foot. See p149 for more on the city's free attractions.

## Tipping

Though a gratuity is sometimes added onto the cheque for you in finer establishments (or touristy ones), it's still standard practice in pubs, cafes and midrange restaurants to add 10% to 15% if service has been good. If your taxi driver is honest and turns on the meter then you should round up the fare at the end of your journey.

it into your own phone is a good idea. Stop into any of the mobile- (cell-) phone service shops downtown to purchase a card and activate the line.

The Czech Republic uses GSM 900, which is compatible with mobile phones from the rest of Europe, Australia and New Zealand but not with

North American GSM 1900 or totally different Japanese phones.

Some North Americans, however, have dual-band GSM 1900/900 phones that do work here; check with your service provider.

### Country & City Codes

The dialling code for the Czech Republic is 420, but there are no area codes inside the country.

All phone numbers have nine digits, which must be always dialled whether calling next door or a distant town. All landline numbers in Prague begin with a 2; mobile numbers begin with a 6 or 7.

### Useful Phone Numbers
**International direct dial code** (☑00)

**Local directory inquiries** (national/international ☑1180/1181)

## Tourist Information

The **Prague Tourism Portal** (☑12 444, 221 714 444 in English; www.praguewelcome.cz) can help with last-minute accommodation and has good maps and detailed brochures. Its main office is next to the Astronomical Clock at **Old Town Hall** (Map p76, C2; Staroměstské náměstí 5; ⊙9am-7pm Mon-Fri, to 6pm Sat & Sun Apr-Oct, 9am-6pm Mon-Fri, to 5pm Sat & Sun Nov-Mar).

Other locations:

**Praha hlavní nádraží** (Map p92, E2; ⊙9am-7pm Mon-Fri, to 6pm Sat & Sun Apr-Oct, 9am-6pm Mon-Fri, to 5pm Sat & Sun Nov-Mar)

**Malá Strana Bridge Tower** (Map p46, D2; Charles Bridge; ⊙10am-6pm Apr-Oct)

**Rytířská 31** (Map p76, D3; ⊙9am-7pm Apr-Oct, to 6pm Nov-Mar)

# Language

Czech belongs to the western branch of the Slavic language family. Many travellers flinch when they see written Czech, but pronouncing it is not as hard as it may seem at first. Most of the sounds in Czech are also found in English, and of the few that aren't, only one can be a little tricky to master – *rzh* (written as ř). Also, Czech letters always have the same pronunciation, so you'll become familiar with their pronunciation really quickly.

With a little practice and reading our pronunciation guides as if they were English, you'll be understood. Just make sure you always stress the first syllable of a word – in italics in this chapter – and pronounce any vowel written with an accent mark over it as a long sound. In this chapter (m/f) indicates masculine and feminine forms.

To enhance your trip with a phrasebook, visit **lonelyplanet.com**. Lonely Planet iPhone phrasebooks are available through the Apple App store.

## Basics

**Hello.**
*Ahoj.*              *uh·hoy*

**Goodbye.**
*Na shledanou.*      *nuh·skhle·duh·noh*

**Excuse me.**
*Promiňte.*          *pro·min'·te*

**Sorry.**
*Promiňte.*          *pro·min'·te*

**Please.**
*Prosím.*            *pro·seem*

**Thank you.**
*Děkuji.*            *dye·ku·yi*

**Yes./No.**
*Ano./Ne.*           *uh·no/ne*

**Do you speak English?**
*Mluvíte*            *mlu·vee·te*
*anglicky?*          *uhn·glits·ki*

**I don't understand.**
*Nerozumím.*         *ne·ro·zu·meem*

## Eating & Drinking

**I'm a vegetarian.** (m/f)
*Jsem vegetarián/*   *ysem ve·ge·tuh·ri·an/*
*vegetariánka.*      *ve·ge·tuh·ri·an·ka*

**Cheers!**
*Na zdraví!*         *nuh zdruh·vee*

**That was delicious!**
*To bylo lahodné!*   *to bi·lo luh·hod·nair*

**Please bring the bill.**
*Prosím*             *pro·seem*
*přineste účet.*     *przhi·nes·te oo·chet*

**I'd like ... , please.** (m/f)
*Chtěl/Chtěla*       *khtyel/khtye·luh*
*bych ..., prosím.*  *bikh ... pro·seem*

| a table for (two) | *stůl* *pro (dva)* | stool pro (dvuh) |
|---|---|---|
| that dish | *ten pokrm* | ten po·krm |
| the drinks list | *nápojový* *lístek* | na·po·yo·vee lees·tek |

## Shopping

**I'm looking for ...**
*Hledám ...*         *hle·dam ...*

**How much is it?**
*Kolik to stojí?*    *ko·lik to sto·yee*

**That's too expensive.**
*To je moc drahé.*   *to ye mots druh·hair*

## Can you lower the price?

Můžete mi
snížit cenu?

moo·zhe·te mi
snyee·zhit tse·nu

## Emergencies

### Help!

Pomoc!

po·mots

### Call a doctor!

Zavolejte
lékaře!

zuh·vo·ley·te
lair·kuh·rzhe

### Call the police!

Zavolejte
policii!

zuh·vo·ley·te
po·li·tsi·yi

### I'm lost. (m/f)

Zabloudil/
Zabloudila
jsem.

zuh·bloh·dyil/
zuh·bloh·dyi·luh
ysem

### I'm ill. (m/f)

Jsem nemocný/
nemocná.

ysem ne·mots·nee/
ne·mots·na

### Where are the toilets?

Kde jsou toalety?    gde ysoh to·uh·le·ti

## Time & Numbers

### What time is it?

Kolik je hodin?    ko·lik ye ho·dyin

### It's (10) o'clock.

Je jedna
hodina.

ye yed·nuh
ho·dyi·nuh

### At what time?

V kolik hodin?    f ko·lik ho·dyin

| | | |
|---|---|---|
| morning | ráno | ra·no |
| afternoon | odpoledne | ot·po·led·ne |
| evening | večer | ve·cher |
| yesterday | včera | fche·ruh |
| today | dnes | dnes |
| tomorrow | zítra | zee·truh |

| | | |
|---|---|---|
| 1 | jeden | ye·den |
| 2 | dva | dvuh |
| 3 | tři | trzhi |
| 4 | čtyři | chti·rzhi |
| 5 | pět | pyet |
| 6 | šest | shest |
| 7 | sedm | se·dm |
| 8 | osm | o·sm |
| 9 | devět | de·vyet |
| 10 | deset | de·set |

## Transport & Directions

### Where's the ...?

Kde je ...?    gde ye ...

### What's the address?

Jaká je
adresa?

yuh·ka ye
uh·dre·suh

### Can you show me (on the map)?

Můžete
mi to ukázat
(na mapě)?

moo·zhe·te
mi to u·ka·zuht
(nuh muh·pye)

### A ticket to ..., please.

Jízdenku
do ..., prosím.

yeez·den·ku
do ... pro·seem

### What time does the bus/train leave?

V kolik hodin
odjíždí
autobus/vlak?

f ko·lik ho·dyin
od·yeezh·dyee
ow·to·bus/vluhk

### Please stop here.

Prosím vás
zastavte.

pro·seem vas
zuhs·tuhf·te

### I'd like a taxi.

Potřebuji
taxíka.

po·trzhe·bu·yi
tuhk·see·kuh

### Is this taxi available?

Je tento taxík
volný?

ye ten·to tuhk·seek
vol·nee

# Behind the Scenes

## Send Us Your Feedback

We love to hear from travellers – your comments help make our books better. We read every word, and we guarantee that your feedback goes straight to the authors. Visit **lonelyplanet.com/contact** to submit your updates and suggestions.

Note: We may edit, reproduce and incorporate your comments in Lonely Planet products such as guidebooks, websites and digital products, so let us know if you don't want your comments reproduced or your name acknowledged. For a copy of our privacy policy visit lonelyplanet.com/privacy.

## Our Readers

Many thanks to the travellers who wrote to us with useful advice and anecdotes:

Tracy, Lòis Armas, Gord Barentsen, Grethe Hansen, Malcolm Hodgson, Kenneth Madsen, Rob Phillips, Thomas Timmermans

## Bridget's Thanks

Thanks to my dear friends, especially Amanda, Elizabeth, Starla, Natalia and Trevor, and my former students. And thanks to Lonely Planet for sending me back to one of my favourite cities.

## Acknowledgments

Cover photograph: Old Town at dusk with the twin towers of the Church of Our Lady Before Týn; Frank Chmura/Getty. Many of the images in this guide are available for licensing from Lonely Planet Images: www.lonelyplanetimages.com.

## This Book

This 3rd edition of *Pocket Prague* was written by Bridget Gleeson. Previous editions were written by Brett Atkinson and Sarah Johnstone. The book was commissioned in Lonely Planet's London office, and produced by the following: **Commissioning Editor** Joe Bindloss **Coordinating Editors** Jackey Coyle, Andrea Dobbin **Coordinating Cartographer** Hunor Csutoros **Coordinating Layout Designer** Frank Deim **Managing Editors** Bruce Evans, Anna Metcalfe **Senior Editors** Susan Paterson, Angela Tinson **Managing Cartographers** David Connolly, Mandy Sierp **Managing Layout Designer** Chris Girdler **Cover Research** Naomi Parker **Internal Image Research** Aude Vauconsant **Language Content** Annelies Mertens **Thanks to** Janine Eberle, Ryan Evans, Victoria Harrison, Liz Heynes, Laura Jane, David Kemp, Alana Mahony, Trent Paton, Piers Pickard, Kirsten Rawlings, Lachlan Ross, Michael Ruff, Julie Sheridan, Laura Stansfeld, John Taufa, Gerard Walker, Clifton Wilkinson

# Index

# Our Writer

### Bridget Gleeson

Before she was paid to travel and write, Bridget made a living teaching English to Czech businessmen. She became acquainted with Prague on early-morning tram rides, sojourns to offices in the suburbs, hours in the city's grand cafes, and Saturdays brightened by snow or sunshine. She writes for Lonely Planet, *Budget Travel*, Jetsetter, BBC Travel, *Afar*, Mr & Mrs Smith and Tablet Hotels.

**Published by Lonely Planet Publications Pty Ltd**
ABN 36 005 607 983
3rd edition – May 2012
ISBN 978 1 74179 924 8
© Lonely Planet 2012   Photographs © as indicated 2012
10 9 8 7 6 5 4 3 2
Printed in China